Life Aboard
a British Privateer

RUNNING PAST MINEHEAD WITH A FINE GALE AT S.E.

Life Aboard a British Privateer

The First Hand Account of a Famous
Privateer Captain at War with the Spanish
During the Reign of Queen Anne 1707-1711

Robert C. Leslie
and

Woodes Rogers

LEONAUR

Life Aboard a British Privateer
The First Hand Account of a Famous Privateer Captain
at War with the Spanish
During the Reign of Queen Anne 1707-1711
by Robert C. Leslie
and
Woodes Rogers

First published under the title
Life Aboard a British Privateer in the Time of Queen Anne

Leonaur is an imprint
of Oakpast Ltd

ISBN: 978-0-85706-298-7 (hardcover)
ISBN: 978-0-85706-297-0 (softcover)

http://www.leonaur.com

Contents

Preface

In offering to English sailors a new edition of the narrative portion of Captain Woodes Rogers' voyage round the world, I have only to say that it is to men of his stamp, in command of small handy seaworthy ships like the *Duke* that England now owes her great "sea power," rather than to the building of large unhandy expensive machines like our present first-class battleships; or even of mosquito-fleets of torpedo boats unable to keep the sea in an ordinary gale of wind. The construction of all such craft is really only a question of money, and may proceed much faster than we can ever hope to breed and train seamen or officers of the Rogers type able to take charge of them.

Steam has of course altered the conditions of life at sea since his time, but the sea has not changed, and the time required to fit a man for service afloat should not be less today than it was in the time of Queen Anne.

Robert C. Leslie.

October, 1893.

The Introduction and Dedication

Most people know their *Robinson Crusoe,* and have heard of the author Defoe. But how many of us have heard even the name of Woodes Rogers, Master Mariner? or have read his quaint *Journal* of a cruising voyage round the world in the ships *Duke* and *Dutchess* of Bristol, "printed in 1712 for A. Bell and B. Lintot at the Crosse Keys and Bible between the two Temple Gates, Fleet Street"? Yet it was this Woodes Rogers who not only discovered the original Crusoe, Alexander Selkirk, but after making a "note of him when found" upon the island of Juan Fernandez,[1] at once proceeded to make very practical use of him by giving him command of the *Increase,* one of many small prizes taken in the South Seas from the Spaniards by the *Duke* and *Dutchess.*

That Rogers was more than a master mariner, of much resource and pluck, is shown in his Journal, and the wonderful way in which he handled the very mixed group of men which formed the small floating commonwealth under him. It was more than thirty years later that Lord Anson sailed a similar voyage round the world with the advantage of the experience of Rogers and others, while Anson's squadron was fitted, manned, and armed by Government: yet, considering the loss of life and material which marked that cruise, it seems to me that, judged by results, Rogers' voyage was a far more wonderful performance, and that it attracted some attention at the time is shown by a notice of it in Captain Berkley's *Naval History* (published, 1756), where, under the heading of *Conduct of the Bristol Privateers,* he says, "We have read in very pompous language the names of those who, with great ships and great preparations, encompassed the Globe. But at this time

---

1. Though this island in the Pacific is the one usually associated with Robinson Crusoe, Defoe conceals its identity by wrecking Crusoe's ship upon an island to the north of Brazil, near the "Great River Oroonoque."

came in two privateers, of Bristol, who with no more than the common strength of such vessels, undertook the voyage, and at the end of two years and three months returned," &c.

In his own Preface, Captain Rogers says, "I was not fond to appear in print; but my friends who had read my journal, prevailed with me at last to publish it," adding, "I know 'tis generally expected, that when far distant voyages are printed, they should contain new and wonderful discoveries, with surprising accounts of people and animals; but this voyage being only designed for cruising on the enemy, it is not reasonable to expect such accounts here as are to be met with in travels relating to history, geography, &c., while, as for stile, I have not had time, were it my talent, to polish it; nor do I think it necessary for a mariner's journal. 'Tis also," he says, "a particular misfortune, which attends voyages to the South Sea, that buccaneers, to set off their own knight-errantry, and to make themselves pass for prodigies of courage and conduct, have given such romantick accounts of their adventures, and told such strange stories, as make the voyages of those who come after (and cannot allow themselves the same liberty), to look flat and insipid to unthinking people.

"Therefore I request my readers, that they be favourable in their censures when they peruse this journal, which is not calculated to amuse, but barely to relate the truth, and which is all written in the language of the sea, that being more genuine and natural for a mariner than the method used by authors that write ashoar."

I have, therefore, in the following extracts, quoted Rogers' *Journal* as closely as possible, adding only a short connecting note here and there, where required. Captain Rogers dedicated his book, "To the worthy Gentlemen my surviving owners, the Worshipfull Christopher Shuter Esq., Sir John Hawkins, Kt, John Romsey, Esq., Captain Philip Freak, Mr. James Hollidge, Francis Rogers, Thomas Goldney, Thomas Clements, Thomas Coutes, John Corseley, John Duckinfield, Richard Hawksworth, William Saunders, John Grant, Lawrence Hollister, and Daniel Hickman, Merchants in Bristol," in these words:

Gentlemen, As you did me the honour to approve my proposals for the following voyage and generously fitted out two ships, in which you gave me the principal command, I no sooner resolved to publish my journal, than I determined to chuse you for my patrons, and thereby to take an opportunity of expressing my gratitude to you, who had the courage to adventure your Estates on an undertaking which to men less discerning seemed impracticable And I make no doubt it will be to your lasting Honour, that such a voyage was undertaken from *Bristol* at your expense; since it has given the publick a sufficient evidence of what may be done in those parts, and since the nation has now agreed to establish a trade to the South Seas, which with the Blessing of God may bring vast riches to Great Britain. I wish you intire Health and happiness, and am.

Gentlemen,

Your most Humble Servant,

Woodes Rogers.

CHAPTER 1

From King Road, Bristol, to Cork in Ireland

1708

Many a modern pleasure yacht would exceed the tonnage of the frigates *Duke* and *Dutchess*, the *Duke* being 320 tons, with 30 guns and 117 men, and the *Dutchess* only 260 tons, with 26 guns, and 108 men. "Both ships," says Rogers, "well furnished with all necessaries on board for a distant undertaking, weighed from King Road, Bristol, August 2nd, 1708, in company with the *Scipio, Peterborough frigot, Prince Eugene, Bristol Galley, Berkley Galley, Bucher Galley, Sherstone Galley*, and *Diamond Sloop*, bound to Cork in Ireland." These "galleys" must not be confounded with the lateen rigged vessels of that name in the south of Europe; being simply small, low, straight ships of light draught easily moved by oars or sweeps in calms.

In Rogers' time a ship was said to be "Frigate built" when she had a poop and forecastle rising a few steps above the waist, and "galley built," when there was no break in the line of her deck and topsides. But the use of oars was not confined to these Bristol[1] galley built ships, for Rogers speaks of using them on several occasions in the *Duke* and *Dutchess*. While in old draughts of small vessels of this class, of even a later date row-ports are often shown.

---

1 Writing of Bristol in 1808, Pinkerton says that "in the late wars with France they built here a sort of galleys, called runners, which being well armed and manned, and furnished with letters of marque, overtook and mastered several prizes of that nation. Many of these *ships* were then also carriers for the London merchants, who ordered their goods to be landed here, and sent to Gloucester by water, thence by land to Lechlade, and thence *down* the Thames to London; the carriage being so reasonable that it was more than paid for by the difference of the insurance and risque between this port and London."

Between the Holmes and Minehead the little fleet came to "an Anchor from 10 to 12 at night, when all came to sail again, running past Minehead with a fine gale at S.E. at six in the morning." No time was lost before an attempt was made to add to the number of the fleet, for the same day, at 5 p.m., the *Dutchess*, like a young hound, breaks away from the pack in chase of what seemed a large ship, which they lost sight of again at 8 o'clock. But "having been informed at Bristol that the *Jersey*, a French man-of-war, was cruising betwixt England and Ireland, the ships sailed all night with hammocks stowed and cleared for a fight. Though it was well for us," says Rogers, "that this proved a false alarm, since had it been real we should have made but an indifferent fight, for want of being better manned."

After parting company with three galleys and the *Prince Eugene*, the fleet, on the 5th of August, "finding they had overshot their port, come to an anchor at noon off two rocks, called the Sovereigne's Bollacks, near Kinsale; at 8 p.m. they weighed again with a small gale at east, which increased and veered to northard." At this time Rogers had a Kinsale pilot on board who, he says, "was like to have endangered our ships by turning us into the next bay to the west of Cork, the weather being dark and foggy."

"Which," says Rogers, "provoked me to chastise him for undertaking to act as pilot without understanding his business better." On the 7th the *Duke* and *Dutchess* anchored in the Cove of Cork, and remained there, more or less weather bound, until the 28th, the entries in Rogers' log varying little beyond telling us that on the 11th, "it blowed fresh and dirty weather:" while on the 12th, "it blew fresh and dirty weather, on which day there cleared and run near forty of our fresh water sailors." In whose place "came off a boat load of men from Cork, that appeared to be brisk fellows but of several nations; so I sent to stop the rest till we were ready, our ships being pestered." On the 28th the weather was fine enough to "Careen clean and tallow the ships five streaks below the water line." Nothing marked the smart privateersman and seaman of those days more than his constant care in keeping the bottom of his ship perfectly clean. Indeed, Captain Rogers never seemed happier than when he had one or other of the little frigates heeld over for scraping and cleaning, in some quiet bay, so nearly upon her beam ends, as to bring her keel almost out of water.

When shipping the rest of his crew before sailing from Cork, we get a taste of Rogers' foresight and policy. For he tells us, "we have now above double the number of officers usual in privateers, besides a

14

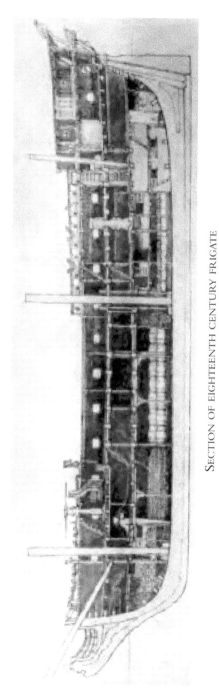

SECTION OF EIGHTEENTH CENTURY FRIGATE

large complement of men;" adding, "we took this method of doubling our officers to prevent mutinies, which often happen in long voyages, and that we might have a large provision for a succession of officers in each ship in case of mortality."

It must, however, have been a sore trial to a tarpaulin seaman, like Rogers, to have to note at the same time, "that in order to make room for our men and provisions, we sent the sheet cable and some other store cordage on shore, having on board three cables besides, and being willing rather to spare that than anything else we had aboard."

In a small frigate quite a fourth part of the hold was, before the introduction of chain cables, occupied by the cable tier or room; and when one considers, not only the space they filled, but the difficulty of handling them, and the care required to keep them from chafing when in use, and from damp and rot when stowed away, it is astonishing that ships returning from long cruises ever had an anchor or cable left which they could trust.

Among the troubles attending the use of hemp cables, that of firing in the hawes holes and at the bits, or timbers they passed over in running out, was one; and each time the anchor was let go men were stationed with buckets of water to prevent this.

It was while victualling and shipping men at this time that a side-note appears of the "Strange behaviour of our men at Cork," alluding to the fact, "that they were continually marrying whilst we staid there, though they expected to sail immediately." Among others, a Dane was coupled by an Irish priest to an Irish woman, without understanding a word of each other's language, so that they were forced to use an interpreter. "Yet," says Rogers, "I perceived this pair seemed more afflicted at separation than any of the rest; the fellow continued melancholy for several days after we were at sea." Whether the Irish bride shared her Danish husband's depression is, of course, not related by Rogers, who goes on to say that "the rest, understanding each other, drank their cans of flip² till the last minute, concluding with a health to our good voyage, and their happy meeting, and then parted unconcerned."

Though the chief command of the expedition fell to Woodes Rogers, master mariner, yet, as was the case in most of these private ventures to the South Seas, several of his officers were men with no claim to the name of sailor, who had either money invested in the ships, or interest with the owners. It is not surprising, therefore, to find

2. "Flipp, a liquor much used in ships, made by mixing beer with spirits and sugar."—Johnson, 1760.

that "the second captain of the *Duke*, and captain of the Marines, was one Thomas Dover,[3] a doctor of phisick," or that this Captain Dover's first lieutenant was "his kinsman, Mr. Hopkins, an apothecary." On the other hand, Rogers had cleverly secured as his master the celebrated William Dampier, also rated "Pilot of the South Seas," "he having," as Rogers says, "already been there three times and twice round the world."

This was no doubt poor Dampier's last venture at sea, for though Rogers mentions his name once or twice in consultation during the cruise, he is altogether lost sight of towards the end of it. Among the other officers, "the third mate, John Ballet, was also designed surgeon, having," says Rogers, "been Captain Dampier's doctor in his last unfortunate voyage;" while two young lawyers have their names upon the ship's books, "designed to act as midshipmen."

Including boatswains, gunners, carpenters, &c., there were on board the *Duke* thirty-six officers, and of the rest of the crew, we are told that "a third were foreigners, while of Her Majestie's subjects many were tailors, tinkers, pedlars, fiddlers, and hay-makers, with ten boys and one negro; with which mixed gang we hope to be well manned as soon as they have learnt the use of arms, and got their sea legs;" which, says Rogers, "we doubt not soon to teach 'em and bring 'em to discipline."

It was the 1st of September before the *Duke* and *Dutchess* left the Cove of Cork with twenty merchant vessels, under convoy of Her Majesty's ship *Hastings*, "both of us," says Rogers "very crowded and pestered ships, their hold full of provisions, and between decks encumbered with cables, much bread, and altogether in a very unfit state to engage an enemy, without throwing many stores overboard." Nevertheless, on the 2nd, the two little frigates stand out from the fleet to chase a sail to windward; and Rogers is glad to find that they sailed as well as any in the fleet, not even excepting the man-of-war, so that, he says, "we begin to hope we shall find our heels, since we go so well though deep and pestered."

The chase, however, proved an inoffensive "French built *Snow*,[4] of

---

3. This Captain or Doctor Thomas Dover was the inventor of the celebrated powders of that name.

4. *Snow*. A vessel which would now be called a brig. The largest two masted craft of that time, and then distinguished from a brig by having a square mainsail below her main topsail; a fore and aft sail being also carried upon a small spar fitted to, and just abaft the mainmast. In the original brigs this fore and aft sail was set upon the mainmast itself, and was the mainsail, in the *Snow* it became the spanker.

CAPTAIN ROGERS'S CARRIAGE STOPS THE WAY

Bristol, joining our fleet from Baltimore" (Ireland).

The weather being fine, on the 4th of September, Rogers and Captain Courtenay of the *Dutchess*, in answer to a signal from Captain Paul, of the Sherstone galley, make a morning call upon that gentleman, in which they are joined by the commander of the *Scipio*, and after being "handsomely treated by Captain Paul," he proposes joining them in a few days, privateering off that well-stocked preserve. Cape Finisterre. A marginal note occurs here in Rogers' journal of "Captain Paul's civility," referring to a present, or tip, "of some scrubbers, and iron scrapers for our ships' bottoms, together with a speaking trumpet and other things we wanted, for which Captain Paul would accept nothing in return."

The time had now come for parting company with the man-of-war, "and it became necessary," says Rogers, "to acquaint the ships companies with our designes in order that while in company with one of Her Majesties ships any malcontents might be exchanged into her. But with the exception of one fellow who expected to have been made tything man in his parish that year, and said his wife would have to pay forty shillings in his abscence, all hands were satisfied," while even the discontented tything man became reconciled to his lot, when asked to join all hands at the grog-tub in drinking to a good voyage. Parting company, however, with the man-of-war also entailed giving up the proposed cruise off Finisterre with the Sherstone Galley, or as Rogers puts it "we had to break measures with Captain Paul. But I excused it to him and saluted him, which he answered and wished us a prosperous undertaking. Wind N. by W. and clear weather."

As the crowded little frigates roll across the Bay of Biscay together before this fair wind, we have the first entry in Captain Rogers' log of one of the many snug little dinners given on board his ship to the officers of the *Dutchess*, and which is returned by them in due form the next day.

This constant interchange of civilities among the officers of ships sailing in company is a very marked feature in the manners and customs of the mariners of that date. Among men-of-war anchored in roadsteads or in port such events are even now, of course, not uncommon. But in those days, judging from entries in Rogers' log, few days passed at sea without actual communication by boat between the ships, the crews of which must have had constant practical experience, both in lowering and hoisting in boats. While, though this must often have been done with a high sea running, there is no record of a mishap to a boat or crew during the entire cruise—a fact speaking volumes for the fine boatmanship of the sailors of this period.[5]

Though practically under the able leadership of Rogers, the two privateers formed together a small floating commonwealth, no important measures being decided upon until they had passed a committee of the officers of both ships. The first of these marine parliaments sat on board the *Duke*; just after, an entry in Rogers' log says, "that now we begin to consider the length of our voyage, and the many different climates we must pass, and the excessive cold which we cannot avoid going about Cape Horn; at the same time we have but a slender stock of liquor, and our men but meanly clad, yet good liquor to sailors is preferable to clothing. Upon this we held our first committee to debate whether t'was necessary for us to stop at Madera?"

Here follows a minute of the resolutions as passed, which are formally signed by each member of the Committee, thus:

Thos: Dover, President.

Stephen Courtenay.	Carleton Vanbrugh.
Woodes Rogers.	Tho: Glendall.
Edward Cooke.	John Bridge.
William Dampier.	John Ballet.
Robert Frye.	

At six the next morning both frigates go in chase of a sail, "the *Dutchess* having a mile start given her in order to spread the more;" Rogers adding "that it blew fresh with a great sea, and the chase being to windward, we crowded extravagantly."

Nine hours later they came up with the chase, "who bore right down upon us, showing Swedish colours. We fired twice at her before she brought to, when we boarded her, Captain Courtney's boat being just before ours. We examined the master, and found he came round Scotland and Ireland."

This was a very usual track in the old war times, in order to avoid capture in the British Channel. But it made Rogers suspect the Swede of having something in the shape of war-like stores on board, so that,

---

5. Forty or fifty years ago the crews of South Sea whalers were very smart sea-boatmen, and their captains thought nothing of lowering a boat in a double reefed topsail breeze, to take a cup of tea or glass of grog with the captain of a ship in company. Great simplicity was the main feature of boat lowering gear on board these ships; but constant practice made communication between them so easy, that it took place often under difficulties which now would be sufficient to entitle the officer in charge of the boat to a gold watch and chain.

22

naturally anxious to prove her a prize, after such a long chase to windward, and believing some men "he found drunk, who told us they had gunpowder and cables aboard, he resolved to strictly examine her, placing twelve men on board, and taking the master and twelve of her men on board the *Duke*." Nothing, however, was found to prove her a prize, and Rogers "let her go," as he says, "without the least embezelment. Her master giving him two hams and some ruffet dried beef," in return for which Rogers gave him "a dozen bottles of red-streak cider."

The characters of both Rogers and crew come out strongly on this occasion, for he tells us "that while I was on board the *Swede* yesterday our men mutinyed. The ringleaders being our boatswain and three inferior officers. But this morning the chief officers having kept with me in the after part of the ship we confined the authors of this disorder, in which there Was not one foreigner concerned, putting ten mutineers in irons, a sailor being first soundly whipped for exciting the rest to join him. Others less guilty were punished and discharged, but I kept the chief officers all armed, fearing what might happen; the ship's company seeming inclined to favour the mutineers, some begged pardon and others I was forced to wink at." The only reason for this rising was discontent of the crew at not being allowed to plunder the *Swede*.

"Two days later," says Rogers, "the men in irons discovered others who were ringleaders in the mutiny." These are, of course, placed in irons with the rest. Captain Rogers judiciously creating a new boatswain, "in the room of Giles Cash, who, being a most dangerous fellow," I agreed with the master of the *Crown Galley*, then in company, to carry for me in irons to Madera, "which extreme measure" was taken because "on September the 14th a sailor followed by near half the ship's company came aft to the steeridge door, and demanded the boatswain out of irons; on which," says Rogers, "I desired him to speak with me on the quarter deck, which he did, where, the officers assisting, I seized him (*i.e.*, tied him up) and made one of his chief comrades whip him, which method I thought best for breaking any unlawful friendship amongst themselves, which, with different correction to other offenders, allayed this tumult, so that now they began to submit quietly and those in irons to beg pardon and promise amendment.

"This mutiny would not have been easily layed were it not for the number of our officers, which we begin to find very necessary to bring our crew to discipline, always difficult in privateers, but without which 'tis impossible to carry on any distant undertaking like ours. Fine pleasant weather, moderate gales." Two days later, "on their humble submission, and strict promise of good behaviour for the time to come," the mutineers are set free; "they having," says Rogers, "while they continued in irons had centries over 'em, and were fed with bread and water."

On September the 18th they sight "Pico Teneriff, and at 5 next morning spyed a sail under their lee bow, which proved a prize, a Spanish *bark* about 25 tuns belonging to Oratava in Teneriff, and bound to Forteventura with about 45 passengers; who rejoiced when they found us English, because they feared we were Turks, Amongst the prisoners were four fryars, one of them the Padre Guardian for the Island of Forteventura, a honest fellow whom we made heartily merry drinking King Charles the *Thirds* health, but the rest were of the *wrong sort.*"

CHAPTER 2

Amongst the Canary Isles

Considering that Captain Rogers' main object in cruising among the Grand Canaries was to lay in a store of liquor for his voyage "about Cape Horn," this small Spanish *bark*, with a cargo of two butts of wine, and a hogshead of brandy, was a lucky windfall.

A trifling hitch occurred, however, about her ransom, owing to the headstrong conduct of Mr. Carlton Vanbrugh, the *Duke's* agent, "who, against his captain's judgement," went ashore with the master of the prize to settle this matter, and was there detained; the authorities refusing to let him go unless the *bark* was restored to them free of charge; they claiming protection from capture for all vessels trading between these islands; which view of the case was supported, not only by the British Consul at Oratava, but by certain English merchants there, and from whom Rogers received a long letter actually advising him to give up his prize; which he answered in full, with his reasons for not doing this; the chief of which was, that possession is nine-tenths of the law.

The answer of the Spanish authorities, however, "being," as Rogers tells us, "of a dilatory character," he at once wrote the following dispatch; informing them "that had it not been out of respect for his officer ashoar, he would not have staid one minute, and that now he should stay only till morning for their answer, taking meanwhile a cruise among the Islands in order to make reprisals, and though he could not land his men, that he would visit the town with his guns by eight next morning; when he hoped to meet the Govenor's Frigot, and repay his civility in his own way."

"Which letter," says Rogers, "had its effect, for as we stood in close to the town at eight o'clock next morning, we spyed a boat coming off, in which proved to be one Mr. Crosse, an English merchant, and our agent Mr. Vanbrugh, with wine, grapes, hogs, and other necessaries for the ransom of the *bark*. And so, upon his coming up, we immediately went to work, discharged the bark, and parted her cargoe between our ships. We treated Mr. Crosse as well as we could, and at his desire, gave the prisoners back as much as we could find? of what belonged to their persons, particularly to the fryars their books. Crucifixes, and reliques. We presented the old *padre* with a cheese, and such as were stripped with other clothes, so that we parted well satisfied on all sides."

After which very comfortable arrangement, Captain Rogers, carefully concealing his destination from the Spaniards by stating that he was "bound to the English West Indies," sailed on his way rejoicing, "that now we are indifferently well stocked with liquors, and shall be better able to endure cold when we get the length of Cape Horn."

On the afternoon of the 22nd "another sail was spyed and chaced to the westward, until, a stiff gale coming on, put us," says Rogers, "out of hopes of seeing her again to advantage." The next day, the weather being fine, with fresh gales, the officers of both ships again dine together on board the *Duke*, when a committee is held and a vote of censure passed upon Mr. Carlton Vanbrugh for landing against the wish of his captain. No doubt also the quality of the Canary was discussed, and perhaps helped to smooth the course of this debate.

It would seem, from the next entry in the log, that the penalties usually exacted by Neptune of those crossing the *Line* for the first time, then became his due somewhat earlier in the voyage; or upon first entering what sailors call the "horse latitudes." For Rogers says that September the 25th "we passed the tropick, and according to custom ducked those that had not done so before. The manner of doing it was by a rope through a block from the main yard to hoist 'em above halfway up to the yard and let 'em fall at once into the water, having a stick cross through their legs, and well fastened to the rope, that they might not be surprised and let go their hold.[1]

"This proved of great use to our freshwater sailors to recover the colour of their skins, which were grown very black and nasty. Those that we ducked after this manner three times were about sixty, and others that would not undergo it chose to pay half a crown fine; the money to be levyed and spent at a public meeting of all the ships companies when we return to England. The Dutchmen and some

---

1. Among old seamen, these duckings, etc., were also inflicted upon those passing the Straits of Gibraltar for the first time.

Englishmen desired to be ducked, some six, others eight, ten, and twelve times, to have the better title for being treated when they come home."

The *Duke* and *Dutchess* made the Island of Sal, one of the Cape de Verds, on the morning of September 29th, and "after being satisfied," says Rogers, "it was Sal, we stood from it W. and W. by N. for St. Vincent, going under easy sail all night because we had none aboard either ship that was acqainted with these islands; but on the 30th when day broke we saw 'em all in a range much as is laid down in the draughts, and at ten o'clock anchored in the bay of St. Vincent in five fathom water." When one considers the means by which these early masters mariners determined their position at sea, and that for want of good timekeepers they were almost quite dependent upon dead reckoning for their longitude, the accuracy and boldness with which Rogers made his landfalls is truly surprising.

The accompanying figures, from a standard work upon navigation of the period,[2] are interesting as showing the curious form of nautical instruments used by old shipmen, like Woodes Rogers, for taking

THE FIGURE OF THE QUADRANT AND
MANNER OF OBSERVATION. (DAVIS'S
QUADRANT.)

2. J. Seller's *Practical Navigation*, 1694.

altitudes of the sun, moon, pole stars, &c., before the invention of Hadley's quadrant.

"Davis's Quadrant," invented by the celebrated navigator of that name in Queen Elizabeth's time, was the best of these. This instrument was known also as "the back-staff" from the position of the observer with his back to the sun when using it. The cross-staff or fore-staff was, however, still used, as it was in the time of Columbus; this was simply a four-sided straight staff of hard wood, about three feet long, having four cross-pieces of different lengths made to slide upon it as the cross-piece does upon a shoemaker's rule.

These cross-pieces were called respectively the ten, thirty, sixty, and ninety cross, and were placed singly upon the staff according to the altitude of the sun or star at time of observation; the angle measured being shown by a scale of degrees and minutes intersected by the cross-piece on that side the staff to which it (the cross) belonged.

THE FIGURE OF THE CROSS-STAFF
AND THE MANNER OF OBSERVATION.

Besides the cross-staff, a form of small quadrant, called an "Almacantas staff," was used just after sunrise and before sunset, for finding the sun's azimuth, and the variation of the compass, while in latitudes north of the line, the "Nocturnal" gave the hour of the night, by observing with it the hands of the great star-clocks, Ursa Major and Minor, as they turned about the pole star.

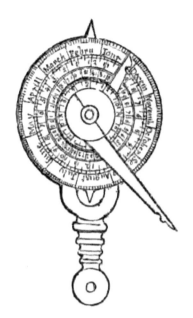

THE FIGURE OF THE NOCTURNAL.

"The day after anchoring at St Vincent," Rogers says, "we cleared our ships, but it blowed too hard to row our boatloads of empty butts ashoar; and we could do little to wooding and watering, till this morning; we were forced to get a rope from the ship to the watering-place, which is a good half mile from our anchorage, and so hauled our empty casks ashoar by boatloads, in order to have 'em burnt and cleaned in the inside, being oil-casks, and for want of cleaning our water stunk insufferably. But borrowing a cooper from the *Dutchess*, and having five of my own, we made quick dispatch."

"We also sent a boat to St. Antonio, with one Joseph Alexander, a good linguist, and a respectful letter to the Govenour, who accounts himself a great man here, though very poor, to get in truck for our prize goods what we wanted; they having plenty of cattel, goats, hogs, fowls, melons, potatoes, limes, ordinary brandy, tobacco, &c." And while here Rogers adds, "that though our people were meanly stocked with clothes, and the *Dutchess's* crew much worse, yet we are both forced to watch 'em, very narrowly, and punished some of 'em, to prevent their selling what they have to the negroes that come over with little things from St. Antonio's."

In his letter to the Governor, Rogers tells him that "as our stay cannot exceed two days, despatch is necessary, and that the bearer can inform his Honour of the publick occurences of Europe. I and the great successes of the Confederate arms against the French and Spaniards, which no doubt must soon be followed with a lasting peace, which God grant."

From an entry in the journal a few days later to the effect "that our boat returned yesterday with two good black cattel, one for each ship, but no news of our linguist;" it appears that worse luck befell him than that which attended Mr Carlton Vanbrugh, or it may be that he took less real interest in the cruise than that gentleman. Whether this was so or not, the officers of both frigates at once agreed, on the return of the boat "with the two good black cattel," that they "had better leave him behind than to wait with two ships for one man that had not followed his orders;" or, as Captain Rogers puts it in a marginal note, "our linguist deserts."

That there was honour as well as method among the leaders in these "undertakings to the South Seas," is clear from the minutes of a debate now held on board the *Duke*, "to prevent those mutinies and disorders amongst the men who were not yet reconciled since the taking of the small Canary prize."

Among these regulations it was agreed "that what is plunder be adjudged by the superior officers and agents in each ship; and that if any person do conceal any plunder exceeding in value one piece of eight, twenty-four hours after capture of a prize, he shall be severely punished and lose his share of the plunder. The same penalty to be inflicted for being drunk in time of action or disobeying his officer's commands, or deserting his post in sea or land service. That public books of plunder are to be kept in each ship, the plunder to be appraised and divided as soon as possible after capture. Every person to be sworn and serched so soon as they shall come aboard, any person refusing, to forfeit his share of the plunder; and that whereas Captain Rogers and Captain Courtney to make both ships companies easy, have given the whole cabin plunder (which in all probability is the major part), to be divided among the crew, it is agreed that the said Captains Woodes Rogers and Steph:

"Courtney, shall have 5 *per cent*, each of 'em over and above their respective shares, &c. That a reward of twenty pieces of eight be given to him that first sees a prize of good value exceeding 50 tuns." Rogers adds that this arrangement was "agreed on in order to make the men easy, without which we must unavoidably have run into such

30

continual scenes of mischief and disorder, which have not only tended to the great hindrance, but generally to the total disappointment of all voyages of this nature, that have been attempted so far abroad in the memory of man."

Hearing nothing more of "their good linguist," the *Duke* and *Dutchess* "came to sail at seven in the evening," of Oct. 8th, from St. Vincent. After having "put the deputy Govenour of S. Antonio (a negro), ashoar, where he must lie in a hole of the rocks, there being no house on that part of the island." In his description of these islands Rogers mentions "that they have here very large spiders, which weave their webs so strong that 'tis difficult to get through 'em, and that the heats are excessive to us who came newly from Europe, so that several of our men began to be sick and were blooded;" while "some of the officers that went ashore a hunting could meet no game but a wild ass, which after a long chase they got within shot and wounded; yet he afterwards held out so as to tire them, and they returned weary and empty handed."

The piety of the expedition appears to have increased steadily as it got further from home, for as they draw near the Equator "in close cloudy weather with squalls of rain," we read how first "having put up the smith's forge, and he began to work on such things as we wanted," that a day or two after "We began to read prayers in both ships, mornings and evenings, as opportunity would permit, according to the Church of England; designing to continue it the term of the voyage."

The number of junior officers on board the frigates was not always unattended with troubles, in all which cases the first remedy tried by Captain Rogers was that of shuffling, or exchanging them from ship to ship. But it is a significant fact that it was the day after a dinner party on board the *Dutchess*, that her captain came on board the *Duke* with his second mate, Mr. Page, desiring to exchange him into the *Duke* in the room of Mr. Ballet. Page, however, who seems to have held views of his own upon this subject, having declined to get into the *Dutchess's* boat, and thereby "caused his superior officer to strike him, whereupon Page struck again and several blows past," was on his arrival on board the *Duke* at once "ordered on the forecastle into the bilboes;[3] where, it being calm, he slipped through the ship's corporal's hands overboard, thinking to swim back to the *Dutchess*. A boat, however, being alongside, he was soon overtaken, brought on board, and lashed

---

3. Bilboes, long bars of iron with shackles sliding on them, and a lock at the end, used to confine the feet of prisoners as the hands are by handcuffs.

to the main geers,[4] where for this, and his abusive language exciting the men to mutiny, he was drubbed and afterwards confined in irons on board the *Duke.*"

A week later Rogers mentions incidentally in his log, "that this morning I let Mr. Page out of irons on his humble submission, and promises of amendment; fair pleasant weather with fresh gales."

On board the *Duke,* however, the bilboes must have been kept in fair working order, with little time to get rusty, for two days after Mr. Page got clear of them, "two persons being accused of concealing a *peruke,* two shirts, and a pair of stockings from the plunder of the Canary *bark,* are found guilty and ordered into them."

Beyond noting what Rogers calls a "turnado" with lightning, "which fell as if it had been liquid," and that "while the storm held, which was not above an hour, the ships even with all sails furled lay along very much," nothing remarkable is recorded after leaving the Cape de Verds until November 16th, when "with a brave breeze at E. they stood in with the land, and suposed it to be the island of Cape Frio on the coast of Brazile." But "the brave breeze" failing them near land, they were two days "towing and rowing the ships," in foggy, rainy weather, before anchoring in the cove off the Isle of Grande, where they designed to wood, water, and careen their frigates.

Terror of past depredations, committed by the French *Corsairs,* had made the Brazilians very suspicious of strangers, and Rogers says "his boat was fired on several times when trying to land with a present to the Govenour of Angre de Reys; but on finding them to be English the fryars begged pardon and invited them to their Convent."

Besides wooding, watering, and careening his frigates, while at the Isle of Grande, Rogers appears to have unrigged the *Duke's* main and fore masts, for he speaks of "seeking for wood to repair our main and fore trustle trees" (supports of the round tops) "which were broke," and that while so engaged "they found abundance of Frenchmen's graves, which the Portuguese told them were those of near half the crews of two great French ships that watered in this place nine months before. But," adds Rogers, "God be thanked ours are very healthy."

The weather is now described as "violent hot," spite of which Rogers speaks of "cleaning one side of the *Dutchess,* on the afternoon of the 24th, and the other side the next morning; giving the ships great

---

4. Main-geers, an assemblage of tackles coming down to the deck at the main mast, by which the mainyard was hoisted or lowered in ships of that time.

lists;[5] and that having men enough, he let the pinnace, with Captain Dover, Mr. Vanbrugh, and others, go whilst the *Duke* was cleaning, to take their pleasure, but to return by twelve o'clock, when we should want our boat. And when they did so, they brought with 'em a monstrous creature, which they had killed, having prickles like a hedgehog, with fur between them, and a head and tail like a monkey's. It stunk," says Rogers, "intolerably, which the Portugeuse told us was only the skin, that the meat of it is very delicious and that they often killed them for the table. But our men, being not yet at very short allowance, none of 'em had stomach good enough to try the experiment, so that we were forced to throw it overboard to make a sweet ship."

That some of those forming the crews of the *Duke* and *Dutchess* should not enjoy their cruising voyage as well as Rogers and his officers did, is not surprising, and this was evidently the case with "Michael Jones and another, two Irish land-men who," says Rogers, "while we lay at the Isle of Grande run into the woods thinking to get away," in spite of the experiences "of two such sparks that run away the day before from the *Dutchess*, and in the night were so frighted with tygers as they thought, but really by monkeys and baboons, that they ran into the water hollowing to the ship till they were fetched aboard again."

Captain Rogers evidently regarded desertion from his ship as an act of foolish ingratitude, and that men incapable of appreciating the advantages of prosecuting to the bitter end a voyage with him to the South Seas deserved the severest form of punishment; for upon recovering these two ungrateful "Irish land-men," a few days later, they were at once "ordered to be severely whipped and put in irons." It was while engaged in intercepting a canoe, suspected of helping these men to escape, that the *Duke's* agent, Mr. Vanbrugh, again got into trouble, through unluckily shooting an "Indian, the property of a certain fryar who owned and steered that canoe."

While, as the friar alleged that "in the confusion," he not only "lost his slave, but gold amounting to £200, and threatened to seek justice in Portugal or England," Rogers was not able, "though he made

5. With two ships sailing in company, careening in port was effected by heaving one of them down to an angle of about forty-five degrees, by tackles attached to her masts and the hull of the other ship. With a single ship, shot and other heavy stores had to be got out and placed in the largest boats, to which the mast tackles were then made fast, also to other boats weighted temporarily with water. Thus Rogers says here that "Nov. 23rd being a fair pleasant day though violent hot, we heeled the *Dutchess* both sides by us;" *i.e., the Duke.*

the 'fryar' as welcom as he could, to reconcile him." A committee of inquiry was therefore wisely called upon Mr. Vanbrugh's conduct in firing, without orders, upon the canoe.

The result of which inquiry was, that after first entering a protest in the ship's books against Mr. Vanbrugh, he was shifted into the *Dutchess*, her agent, Mr. Bathe, taking his place on board the *Duke*.

Having completed their refit in rather less than a week, which, as it included the lifting of the rigging of the *Duke's* main and fore mast, beside the wooding, watering, and careening of both frigates under a tropical sun, was not bad work; they wound up their stay at the Isle de Grande, by "assisting with both ship's musick," at an important religious function, or, as Rogers calls it, "entertainment," at Angre de Reys; "where," he says, "we waited on the Govenour, Signior Raphael de Silva Lagos, in a body, being ten of us, with two trumpets and a *hautboy*, which he desired might play us to church, where our musick did the office of an organ, but separate from the singing, which was by the fathers well performed.

"Our musick played 'Hey boys up go we!' and all manner of noisy paltry tunes. And after service, our musicians, who were by that time more than half drunk, marched at the head of the company; next to them an old father and two fryars carrying lamps of incense, then an image dressed with flowers and wax candles, then about forty priests, fryars, &c., followed by the Govenour of the town, myself, and Captain Courtney, with each of us a long wax candle lighted. The ceremony held about two hours; after which we were splendidly entertained by the fathers of the Convent, and then by the Govenour. They unanimously told us they expected nothing from us but our Company, and they had no more but our musick."

The day after, however, before sailing, Rogers in return, entertained the Governor and fathers on board the *Duke*, "When," he says, "they were very merry, and in their cups proposed the Pope's health to us. But we were quits with 'em by toasting the Archbishop of Canterbury; and to keep up the humour, we also proposed William Pen's health, and they liked the liquor so well, that they refused neither;" while as "in the evening it came on blowing with thick showers," the Governor, the fathers and friars, made a night of it on board the frigates, not being landed till next morning, "when we saluted 'em with a huzza from each ship, because," as Rogers says, "we were not overstocked with powder, and made them a handsome present of butter and cheese from both ships in consideration of the small presents and

CAPTAIN ROGERS GIVES THE DUKE A GREAT LIST.

yesterday's favours from 'em, and as a farther obligation on 'em to be careful of our letters, which we took this opportunity to deliver into their own hands."

Captain Rogers was evidently well read in all the old 16th and 17th century voyages of the Portuguese, Spaniards, and Dutch; and pages of his book are filled with quotations from them relating to the climate, natural history, and people of the places he touched at. But he is careful also to tell us how far his own observations agreed with these accounts. Thus at Grande he says, "that having Newhoff's account of Brazile on board he found by enquiry and observation his description of the products and animals to be just. Particularly of that monster call the roe-buck serpent, which I enquired after thinking it to be incredible till the Portuguese Govenor told me there are some of them 30 foot long as big as a barrel, and devour a roe-buck at once, from whence they had their name; and that one was killed near this place a little before our arrival."

"The natives of Brazil," Rogers goes on to say, "live in huts built of stakes and covered with Palm leaves, their dishes and cups are calabashes or the shells of a sort pompion, their furniture is hammocks of cotton-like net-work, these they use for beds when they travel, tying them to trees. The women follow their husbands to war and elsewhere, and carry their luggage in a basket with a child hung about them in a peece of callico, a parrot or an ape in one hand; while the idle lubber carries nothing but his arms. They know nothing of arithmetick, but count their years by laying by a chestnut in the season. They fancy that after Death they are transplanted into Devils, or enjoy all sorts of pleasures in lovely fields beyond the mountains, if they have killed and eat many enemies. But those that never did anything of any moment, they say are to be tormented by Devils."

After a long account of the River Amazon, which Rogers says "was not so called because of any nation of Viragos etc," he winds up a long description of the river La Plata with a curious account of stones which breed in an oval case about the bigness of a man's head, which lying underground until they come to maturity break with a noise like bombs, and scatter abundance of beautiful stones of all colours; which at first the Spaniards took to be of great value, but did not find them so."

CHAPTER 3

From Grande Towards Juan Fernandez

Voyage of near 6,000 miles now awaited the little frigates before reaching Juan Fernandez, the first place they expected to refresh at after leaving the Isle de Grande. A good stock of necessaries was, therefore, laid in here, and a letter, giving an account of their proceedings so far, left with the Governor of Angre de Reys, to be sent to England by the first opportunity.

They did not clear the Brazilian coast until December 3rd, and little is recorded in Rogers' journal until the 6th, when, in close, cloudy weather,

At length did cross an albatross,
Thorough the fog it came.

Rogers[1] spells it "Alcatros, a large bird," he says, "who spread their wings from eight to ten feet wide."

The whole of this part of the voyage might, indeed, be described in quotations from the *Ancient Mariner,* for we read that, December the 13th, "in the afternoon the little *Duke's* mainsail was reefed, which was the first time since we left England." For

Now the storm blast came, and he
Was tyrannous and strong;
He struck with his overtaking wings.

---

1 The name of this bird has been said to have been derived from "*alb,*" a priest's white vestment. But Rogers' spelling of the word is no doubt right, "Alcatraz "being the Spanish and Portuguese name for a pelican, and the word was extended by them to any large waterfowl. The word is said to be derived from Arabic, and to signify the leathern bucket of a wheel used for irrigation; which the enormous pouch of the pelican was thought to resemble.

The bird "Alcatros"

And chased us south along.
Again,
And now there came both mist and snow.
And it grew wondrous cold.

Or, as Rogers says, "We find it much colder in this latitude than in the like degree North, though the sun is in its furthest extent to the southard, which may be ascribed to our coming newly out of warmer climates, or 'tis probable the winds blow over larger tracts of ice than in the same degree of N. latitude."

Then we read of thick fog, in which they lose sight of their consort for many hours, "though we made all the noise agreed on between us." And so the monotonous sea-life wears on, varied only by the smallest events, as when, December 10th, the commanders agree to chop boatswain's mates, the *Dutchess* "being mutinous, and they willing to be rid of him." Or how, on the 18th, "in cold hazy rainy weather, one of the men on board the *Dutchess* fell out of the mizen top, and broke his skull," and Captain Rogers boards her "with two surgeons; where they examine the wound, but found the man irrecoverable, so he died, and was buried next day; brisk gales from W.N.W.," &c.

On the 23rd high distant land is sighted, "which appeared first in three, afterwards in several more islands. This," says Rogers, "is Falkland's Land, described in few draughts, and none lay it down right, though the Latitude agrees pretty well." On Christmas Day, blowing a strong gale S.W., at six in the evening they lost sight of the land, but spying a sail under their lee bow, distant four leagues, "immediately," says Rogers, "let our reefs out, chased, and got ground of her apace, till ten at night, when we lost sight of her. We spoke our consort, and agreed to bear away to the northward till dawning, as we were both of opinion, that, if homeward bound, the chase, after loosing sight of us, would steer north. But when it was full light we saw nothing, being thick hazy weather, till 7 a.m.

"When it cleared we saw the chase again, and, falling calm, we both got out our *oars*, rowed and towed with boats ahead, and gained on the chase, till six in the evening; perceiving we approached her, I went in my boat to speak with Captain Courtney, and agree how to engage her if a great ship, as she appeared to be, and adjusted signals, if either of us should find it proper to board her in the night. On returning on board a breeze sprang, and we made all possible sail, keeping the chase in view 'till ten o'clock, when it came on thick again, but, being short nights, we thought it impossible to lose one another, and kept her open on our larboard, and the *Dutchess* on our starboard bow. At one in the morning I was persuaded to shorten sail for fear of losing our consort if we kept on. At daylight it was a thick fog, so that we could see neither our consort nor chase for an hour, when it cleared, and we saw our consort on our larboard bow, and fired a gun for her to bear down, but we immediately saw the chase ahead of the *Dutchess* a few miles, which gave us new life.

"We forthwith haled up for them, but the wind heading us, we had a great disadvantage in the chase. The water was smooth however. And we ran at a great rate, until it coming on to blow more and more, the chase outbore our consort, so she gave off, and being to windward, came down very melancholy to us, supposing the chase to have been a French homeward bound ship from the South Seas.[2] Thus this ship escaped, which considering that we always outwent her before, is as strange as our first seeing of her in this place, because all ships that we have heard of, bound either out or home, keep within Falkland's Island."

Woodes Rogers was no doubt a very hard-headed mariner, still few sailors are without a trace of superstition, and his closing remark, in describing this long and unsuccessful chase, points to a feeling with him that the vessel which all at once "out-bore his consort," was one, the speed and presence of which in that sea was to him a mystery. His own ships were clean, and sailing their best; but very few English vessels of that time were able to "out-go" the ships then built by the French for trade, or piracy, in the South Seas.

The usual foul weather, at any rate, came upon them at once, when,

With far-heard whisper, o'er the sea
Off shot the spectre-bark,

in the shape of "strong gales with heavy squalls from south to west," during which the *Dutchess* (to ease and stiffen her) "put the guns into the hold again that she took up in the chase." Christmas Day, and those following it, must have been days of "toil and trouble" on board the *Duke* and *Dutchess* to both men and officers; but Rogers made up for it all when, "in fresh gales of wind from W.N.W. with fogs, being New Year's Day, every officer was wished a 'Merry New Year' by our own

2. Curiously enough, on his return home, Rogers learnt that this French ship, which so mysteriously "outwent them," was the very vessel in which Captain Stradling, of the *Cinque Ports* (Selkirk's ship), returned to England after being kept four years prisoner by the Spaniards.

musick, and I had a large tub of punch hot upon the quarter-deck, where every man in the ship had above a pint to his share, and drank our owners and friends' healths in Great Britan, to a happy new-year, a good voyage, and a safe return. After which we bore down to our consort, and gave them three huzzas, wishing them the same."

Though, like most good seamen, Woodes Rogers appears to have been lucky in his weather, and during the three years' cruise to have sustained little damage from storm or tempest, the *Duke* and *Dutchess* did not escape a few hours' dusting in the passage "about Cape Horn," for in latitude 60.58 S., on the 5th of January, just past noon, "it came on to blow strong," when Rogers says, "we got down our foreyard and reefed our foresail and mainsail; but there came on a violent gale of wind and a great sea. A little before 6 p.m. we saw the *Dutchess* lowering her mainyard. The tack flew up, and the lift unreeved, so that the sail to leeward was in the water and all aback, their ship taking in a great deal of water to leeward. Immediately they loosed their spritsail, and wore her before the wind. I wore after her, expecting when they had gotten their mainsail stowed, they would take another reef in, and bring to under a two reefed mainsail and reefed and ballanced mizen. But to my surprise they kept scudding to southward.

"I dreaded running amongst ice, because it was excessive cold; so I fired a gun as a signal for them to bring to, and brought to ourselves again under the same reefed mainsail. They kept on, and our men reported an ensign in their maintopmast rigging as a signal of distress, which made me doubt they had sprung their mainmast.

"So I wore again, our ship working exceeding well in this great sea. Just before night I was up with them again, and set our fore-sail twice reefed to keep 'em company, which I did all night. About three the next morning it grew more moderate; we soon after made a signal to speak with them, and at five they brought to. When I came within haile I enquired how they all did aboard?

"They answered they had shipped a great deal of water in lying by, and were forced to put before the wind, and the sea had broke in the cabin windows, and over their stern, filling their steerage and waste, and had like to have spoiled several men. But God be thanked, all was otherwise indifferent well with 'em, only they intolerably cold and everything wet."

The next day the weather was raw cold and rainy with a great sea from N.W., which did not, however, deter Rogers and Captain Dampier from "going in the yall on board the *Dutchess* to visit 'em after the storm, where," he says, "we found 'em in a very orderly pickle; with all their clothes drying, the ship and rigging covered with them from the deck to the main-top, while six more guns are got into the hold to make the ship more lively." That so far the *Duke* and *Dutchess*, spite of their small size and number of men (333), were healthy ships, is shown by an entry here in the log of the death of "John Veal, a landman, being the first death from sickness out of both ships since our leaving England." After running as far south as lat. 61.53, "which," says Rogers, "for ought we know is the furthest that anyone has yet been to the southward, and where we have no night;" they, on the 15 of Jan., in longitude 79.58 from London, "accounted themselves in the South Sea, being got round Cape Horn."

Ten days later, the *Dutchess* speaks the *Duke* to the effect that her men are greatly in want of a harbour to refresh them, many being ill through want of clothes, and being often wet in the cold weather. Matters were not much better on board the *Duke*; "several of ours," says Rogers, "being very indifferent. So that as we are very uncertain of the latitude of Juan Fernandez, the books laying 'em down so differently that not one chart agrees with another, and being but a small island, and in some doubts of striking it, we designe to hale in for the mainland to direct us." At seven in the morning, however, of January 31st, 1709, all their doubts were set at rest, and the foundation laid, upon which the *Life and Surprising Adventures of Robinson Crusoe* are built, when Captain Rogers made Juan Fernandez, bearing W.S.W., distant about seven leagues.

The next day at 2 p.m., Rogers says, "we hoisted our pinnace out, and Captain Dover with the boats crew went in her to go ashoar, though we could not be less than four leagues off.

"As soon as it was dark we saw a light ashore; and our boat being then about a league from the island bore away for the ships when she saw the light, and we put out lights for the boat, though some were of opinion the light we saw was our boat's. But as night came on it appeared too large for that. So we fired one quarter deck gun, and several muskets, showing lights in our shrouds, that our boat might find us, whilst we plyed in the lee of the Island.

"About two in the morning our boat came on board, having been in tow of the *Dutchess*; and we were glad they got well off, because it began to blow. We were all convinced this light was on shore, and designed to make our ships ready to engage, believing them to be French ships at anchor, which we must either fight, or want water,"

THE DUTCHESS IN DIFFICULTIES

&c. The next morning "we tacked, to lay the land close aboard, and about ten opened the south end of the island; here the flaws came heavy off shore, and we were forced to reef our topsails. When we opened the middle bay, where we expected to find our enemy, we saw all clear, and no ships in that nor the next bay. Though we guessed there had been ships there, but that they were gone on sight of us. About noon we sent our yall ashore with Captain Dover, Mr. Frye, and six men, all armed; meanwhile we and the *Dutchess* kept turning to get in, and such heavy flaws came off the island that we were forced to let fly our topsail sheets, keeping all hands to stand by our sails for fear of the winds carrying 'em away: though when the flaws were gone we had little or no wind.

"Our boat not returning we sent our pinnace, also armed, to see what was the occasion of the yall's stay; for we were afraid that the Spaniards had a garison there and might have seized 'em. We put out a signal, and the *Dutchess* showed a French ensign. Immediately our pinnace returned from the shore, and brought abundance of craw-fish with a man clothed in goat-skins, who looked wilder than the first owners of them. He had been on the island four years and four months, being left there by Captain Stradling in the ship *Cinque Ports*. His name was Alexander Selkirk, a Scotchman, who had been master of the *Cinque Ports*, a ship that came here last with Captain Dampier, who told me this was the best man in her; so I immediately agreed with him to be mate on board our ship.

"'Twas he made the fire last night when he saw our ships, which he judged to be English. During his stay here he had seen several ships pass, but only two came to anchor, which as he went to view he found to be Spanish and retired from 'em, upon which they shot at him. Had they been French, he would have submitted, but chose to risque dying alone" (note, not living alone) "in the iland, rather than fall into the hands of the Spaniards in these parts, lest they murder, or make a slave of him in the mines; for he feared they would spare no stranger that might be capable of discovering the South Sea.

"The Spaniards he said had landed before he knew what they were, and came so near him that he had much ado to escape: for they not only shot at him, but pursueed him into the woods, where he climbed a tree, at the foot of which they stopped and killed several goats just by, but went off again without discovering him. He told us he was born at Largo in the county of Fife, Scotland, and was bred a sailor from his youth. The reason of his being left here was a difference betwixt him and his captain. When left, he had with him his clothes and bedding, with a firelock, some powder, bullets, and tobacco, a hatchet, a knife, a kettle, a Bible, some practical pieces, and his mathematical instruments and books.

"He diverted and provided for himself as well as he could; but for the first eight months had much ado to bear up against melancholy, and the terror of being alone in such a desolate place. He built two huts with *piemento* trees, covered them with long grass, and lined them with the skins of goats which he killed with his gun as he wanted, so long as his powder lasted, which was but a pound, and that being near spent, he got fire by rubbing two sticks of *piemento* wood together on his knees. In the lesser hut, at some distance from the other, he dressed his vituals, and in the larger he slept, and employed himself in reading, singing Psalms, and praying, so that he said he was a better Christian while in this solitude, than ever he was before, or than he was afraid he should ever be again. At first he never eat anything till hunger constrained him, partly for grief, and partly for want of bread and salt; nor did he go to bed till he could watch no longer. The *piemento*[3] wood, which burnt very clear, served him both for fire and candle, and refreshed him with its pleasant smell.

"He might have had fish enough, but could not eat 'em, as for want of salt,[4] they made him ill, except Crawfish, which are there as large as lobsters and very good. These he sometimes boiled, and at others broiled as he did his goat's flesh, of which he made very good broth, for they are not so rank as ours; he kept an account of 500 that he killed while there, and caught as many more, which he marked on the ear and let go.[5] When his powder failed he took them by speed of foot; for his way of living, and continued exercise of walking and running, cleared him of all gross humours, so that he run with wonderful swiftness through the woods, and up the rocks and hills, as we perceived when we employed him to catch goats for us. We had a bull dog, which we sent with several of our nimblest runners to help him catch goats; but he distanced and tired both the dog and men, catched the goats and brought 'em to us on his back.

---

3. The Allspice tree of the West Indies. This tree usually grows from seed eaten and carried by birds, which easily accounts for its being found upon this island.

4. It seems strange that Selkirk never thought of making salt by evaporating sea water.

5. Thirty years later Commodore Anson found some of Selkirk's ear-marked goats when he touched at Juan Fernandez.

JUAN FERNANDEZ

"He told us that his agility in pursuing a goat had once like to have cost him his life; he pursueed it with so much eagerness that he catched hold of it on the brink of a precipice hidden by some bushes, so that he fell with the goat down the said prescipice a great height, and was so stuned and bruised with the fall that he narrowly escaped with his life, and when he came to his senses found the goat dead under him. He lay there about 24 hours and was scarce able to crawl to his hut a mile distant, or to stir abroad again in ten days. After a while he came to relish his meat well enough without salt and bread, and in the season had plenty of good turnips which had been sowed there by Captain Dampier's men, and have overspread some acres of ground. He had enough of good cabbage from the cabbage trees and seasoned his meat with the fruit of the *piemento* tree, which is the same as the Jamaica pepper and smells deliciously.

"He soon wore out all his shoes and clothing by running through the woods; and at last, being forced to shift without them, his feet became so hard that he run everywhere without annoyance, and it was some time before he could wear shoes after we found him. For not being used to any so long, his feet swelled when he first came to wear 'em. After he conquered his melancholy he diverted himself sometimes by cutting his name on the trees, and the time of his being left and continuance there. He was at first much pestered with cats and rats, that bred in great numbers from some of each species which had got ashore from ships that put in there to wood and water. The rats knawed his feet and clothes while asleep, which obliged him to cherish the cats with goats flesh; by which many of them became so tame that they would lie about him in hundreds, and soon delivered him from the rats.

"He likewise tamed some kids, and to divert himself would now and then sing and dance with them and his cats; so that by the care of Providence, and vigour of his youth, being now about 30 years old, he came at last to conquer all the inconveniences of his solitude and to be very easy. When his clothes wore out he made himself a coat and cap of goatskins, which he stitched together with little thongs of the same that he cut with his knife. He had no other needle but a nail, and when his knife was wore to the back, he made others as well as he could of iron hoops that were left ashore, which he beat thin and ground upon stones. Having some linen cloth by him, he sowed himself shirts with a nail and stitched 'em with the worsted of his old stockings, which he pulled out on purpose. He had his last shirt on

51

when we found him.

"At his first coming on board us," says Rogers, "he had so much forgot his language for want of use, that we could scarce understand him, for he seemed to speak his words by halves. We offered him a dram, but he would not touch it, having drank nothing but water since his being there, and 'twas some time before he could relish our victuals. He could give us an account of no other product of the Island except some small black plums, which are very good, but hard to come at, the trees which bear 'em growing on high mountains and rocks. The climate is so good that the trees and grass are verdant all the year. He saw no venomous or savage creature, nor any sort of beast but goats on the Island. The first of these having been put ashore here on purpose for a breed, by Juan Fernandez, a Spaniard, who settled there with some families till the continent of Chili began to submit to the Spaniards, which tempted them to quit this island, though capable of maintaining a number of people, and of being made so strong that they could not easily be dislodged.

"Ringrose, in his account of Captain Sharp's voyage and other buccaneers, mentions one who had escaped ashore here out of a ship, which was cast away with her company, and says he lived five years alone before he had an opportunity of another ship to carry him off. While Captain Dampier talks of a Moskito Indian that belonged to Captain Watlin, who being a hunting in the woods when the Captain left the island, lived here three years alone, and shifted much as Mr. Selkirk did, till Captain Dampier came hither in 1684 and carryed him off; the first that went ashore was one of his countrymen and they saluted one another, first by prostrating themselves by turns on the ground, and then embracing.

"But whatever there is in these stories this of Mr, Selkirk I know to be true, and his behaviour afterwards gives me reason to believe the account he gave me how he spent his time, and bore up under such an affliction, in which nothing but the Divine Providence could have supported any man. And by this we may see, that solitude and retirement from the world is not such an unsufferable state of life as most men imagine, especially when people are fairly called, or thrown into it unavoidably, as this man was, who in all probability must otherwise have perished in the seas, the ship which he left being cast away not long after, when few of the company escaped. We may perceive also by his story," adds Rogers, "the truth of the maxim *that necessity is the mother of invention*, since he found means to supply his wants in a very natural

MR SELKIRK JOINS THE DUKE FRIGATE

manner, so as to maintain life, though not so conveniently, yet as effectually as we are able to do with the help of all our arts and society.

"It may likewise instruct us how much a plain and temperate way of living conduces to the health of the body and the vigour of the mind, both which we are apt to destroy by excess and plenty, especially of strong liquor. For this man, when he came to our ordinary method of diet and life, though he was sober enough, lost much of his strength and agility. But I must quit these reflections, which are more proper for a philosopher and divine than a mariner, and return to my own subject." Which he does, and at once goes on to tell how "this morning we cleared ship, unbent our sails, and got them ashoar to mend and make tents for our men, while the Govenour, for so we called Mr. Selkirk, (though we might as well have named him *absolute Monarch* of the island,) caught us two goats, which make excellent broth mixed with turnip tops and other greens for our sick, they being twenty in all, but not above two that we account dangerous."

Selkirk kept up this supply, of two goats a day, during the time the ships remained at Juan Fernandez; and no doubt the poor half-wild sailor man rather enjoyed these last goat-hunts before he became absorbed into the busy monotony of sea life on board Rogers' little frigate. We seldom catch Captain Rogers giving himself time for repose during his cruise, but the natural charms of this island appear to have had some effect even upon his practical matter of fact temperament, for he says, while here, "'twas very pleasant ashoar among the green *piemento* trees, which cast a refreshing smell. Our house being made by putting a sail round four of 'em, and covering it a top with another; so that Captain Dover and I both thought it a very agreable seat, the weather being neither too hot nor too cold."

Rogers, however, did not come about the Horn into the South Seas to sit under the shade of sweet-smelling trees, especially after having "been informed at the Canaries, that five stout French ships were coming together to these seas"; therefore, having completed the wooding and watering of his ships, and the boiling down of about eighty gallons of sea-lions' oil,[5] which, he says, "we refined and strained to save our candles, or for the sailors to fry their meat in for want of

---

5. The shores of Juan Fernandez were described by Selkirk at that time, to be swarming with seals, especially in the month of November, or breeding season; when they lay so thick that it was impossible to pass through them, and that they run at a man like an angry dog even when beaten away with a good stick, and Rogers adds, "that when we came in they kept up a continual noise day and night; bleeting like lambs, howling like dogs or wolves, with (continued next page.)

butter," he is, just eleven days after making the island, ready for sea again, with its *"absolute Monarch"* aboard.

Before sailing, however, certain signals, to be made by the arrangement of their sails, were agreed upon between the commanders as to the chasing of ships, &c., while in case of the frigates being separated before reaching their next place of refreshment, the island of Lobos de la Mer, it was settled that "two crosses were to be set up there at the landing place near the farther end of the starboard great island: and a glass bottle to be buried direct north of each cross, with news of what had happened since parting, and their further designes." Nothing indeed now appears to have been left undone which could add to the safety and efficiency of the small force under Rogers' command.

"For a fortnight after leaving Juan Fernandez," he says, "we put both pinnaces in the water to try them under sail, having fixed them each with a gun after the manner of a *patterero*, and all things necessary for small privateers, hoping they'll be serviceable to us in little winds to take vessels": and a few days later in a calm both frigates are again heeled and tallowed, though the nearest land was sixty miles distant; while the crews are put upon an allowance of water of three pints a man per day, "that," says Rogers, "we may keep at sea some time without being discovered by watering ashore. Because an enemy once discovered, there was nothing of any value put to sea from one end of the coast to the other."

It was now the 9th of March, and in fair weather, before a moderate gale at S.E., the ships are kept under easy sail, with all boats in tow, about twenty-one miles off the coast of Peru, "in hopes of seeing rich ships either going or coming out of Lima; the men beginning to repine, that though come so far we have met with no prizes in these seas," which may have accounted for the frigates being brought to for a day at this time, while the men are "sent in the boats under the shoar to examine two white rocks which at a distance looked like ships."

On the 16th, however, a small prize of sixteen tons, manned by two Spaniards and some Indians, falls into their hands, and Rogers learns from these Spaniards that no enemy has been in those parts

---

other hideous noises which could be heard on board a mile from shore." Another "strange creature" described here, is "the sea-lion, some of them 20 foot long and not less than two tun weight; not unlike the sea-dogs or seals, but have another sort of skin with much bigger heads, large mouths, and monstrous big eyes, the face like a lion with very large whiskers the hair of which is stiff enough to make toothpickers."

CAPTAIN ROGERS AND DOVER UNDER THE PIEMENTO TREES

since Captain Dampier was there four years ago; also that Stradling's ship, the *Cinque Ports*, "who was Dampier's consort, foundered on the coast of Barbacour, only Captain Stradling and six or seven men being saved, who lived four years prisoners at Lima much worse than our Govenour Selkirk whom they left on Juan Fernandez."

The following day, piloted by the crew of their prize, they anchored in the "Thorow-fair between the islands of Labos de la Mer," and Rogers, finding his new prize well built for sailing, at once resolved to fit her out as a privateer. She was therefore taken "into a small round cove in the southermost island, hauled up dry, and after having her bottom well cleaned, relaunched, and called the *Beginning*, Captain Cook being appointed to command her."

In the meantime, while Rogers stayed to overlook this, and the building of a "larger boat for landing men, should an attempt be made upon the mainland," the *Dutchess*, having landed her sick men, and been heeled and cleaned outside, is sent upon a cruise round the island, with instructions to meet the *Beginning*, when ready, off the southernmost end of it. Like a true seaman Captain Rogers appears to have thoroughly enjoyed this work of fitting out his "small *bark*," and describes how he got a spare topmast out of the *Duke*, "which made her a new main mast, a mizen topsail being altered to make her a mainsail." And though the work included "fixing a new deck with four swivel guns," she was "victualed and manned by twenty men from the *Duke*, and 12 from the *Dutchess*, all well armed, and ready for sea," in three days from the time of being taken in hand.

"As I saw her out of harbour," says Rogers, proudly, "with our pinnace she looks very pretty and I believe will sail well in smooth water, having all masts, sails, rigging and materials like one of the half galleys fitted out for Her Majestie's service in England."[6]

Two days after joining the *Dutchess*, this pretty little *Beginning* captured another small prize, the *Santa Josepha*, "of 50 tuns, A prize, full of timber, cocou, and cocounuts and some tobacco, which we distributed among our men." And after being cleaned and re-christened the *Increase*, the *Santa Josepha* became the hospital ship of the fleet, "all the sick men and a doctor from each ship being put on board with Mr.

---

6. The "half galley" of the Mediterranean was a vessel of about 120 feet long by 18 wide, and 9 or 10 deep, fitted with two large lateen sails, and masts that could be lowered on deck at pleasure. She carried five cannon, and was rowed with twenty oars on a side. Her English Majestie's galleys and half-galleys were, however, square rigged as small ships or *barks*.

Selkirk as master."

Rogers gives a long account of the adjacent coast and country of Chili, which he says "lies nearest to those who shall think fit to attempt a trade from England to the South Sea." He is told, "that the name of this country in the native language signifies cold, which is so excessive in the mountains called Sierra Nevada, a part of the Cordillera, as to freez men and cattle to death and to keep their corps from putrefaction," while the passage over these mountains toward Cusco is attended with "shortness of breath, reachings, and vomitings; that sixteen vulcanos are, found in this chain which at times break out with dreadful effect, cleaving rocks, and issuing quantities of fire with a noise like thunder. While there are meteors in the air so high at times as to resemble stars, at others so low that they frighten the mules, and buz about their feet and ears."

Among the birds we are told of the "*pinguedas*" (humming birds), whose body is of the size of an almond, or of a big bee, and shines like polished gold mixed with green: the males having a lively orange colour like fire on their heads, and some with tails a foot long. Besides these there are certain sorts of shell-fish upon the coast called Sea stars, others suns, moons, etc., because they resemble those planets as usually painted; which fish being reduced to powder, and drank in wine, are an infallible remedy against drunkenness, and frequently used for that end, because it creates an abhorrence of wine, says "Father Ovalle a native of this country and procurant for it at Rome," and from whom Rogers quotes largely in that portion of his book called "Chili described."

PINNACES UNDER SAIL

CHAPTER 4

From Lobos Toward Guiaquil in Peru

Having given his ship the usual "good heel," and "tallowing her low down," Rogers came to sail March 30th, at ten o'clock, with his new launch in tow from Lobos. On more than one occasion Rogers shows a decided want of sympathy with the sportsmen of the expedition, and relates here "how there were in this island abundance of vultures, alias carrion crows, which looked so like turkeys that one of our officers at landing blessed himself at the sight, hoping to fare deliciously. He was so eager he would not stay till the boat could put him ashore, but leaped into the water with his gun, and getting near to a parcel let fly at 'em. But when he came to take up his game, it stunk insufferably and made us merry at his mistake."

These birds were no doubt a flock of Gallenazo, described by Darwin as frequenting the wooded isles on the west coast of South America, and as "feeding exclusively upon what the sea throws up, and the carcases of dead seals," which, from the following entry in the journal must have been very plentiful in this island, "where," says Rogers, "owing to the presence of certain unwholesome old seals, whose livers disagreed with those of our crew that eat them; the air, with the wind off shore, is loaded with an ugly noisome smell, which gave me a violent headache, and was complained of by all," as quite unlike the spice-laden breezes of Juan Fernandez. Rogers' headache, and these unwholesome old seals, were no doubt quickly forgotten at sea, when listening to the stories of their Spanish prisoners about "a certain rich widow of the late Vice Roy of Peru, who was expected to embark with her family and wealth shortly for Aquapulco. Also of a stout ship with dry goods for Lima, and another richly laden from

Panama, with a Bishop aboard."

Acting on which advice, "it was agreed to spend as much time as possible cruising off Payta without discovering themselves." They had not long to wait, for two days after leaving Lobes "a sail was spyed to windward about daybreak, and the pinnace being hoisted out and manned under the command of Mr. Frye, first lieutenant of the *Duke*, by 8 o'clock took the *Ascension* of 500 tons, built gallion fashion very high with galleries." This was "the stout ship from Lima," and from her "they learnt that the ship with the Bishop would stop at Payta to recruit," and, being near that place, Rogers "resolved to watch narrowly, in order to catch his Lordship."

With the exception of a "small vessel of 35 tuns laden with timber from Guiaquil," and captured by the *Beginning*, nothing hove in sight for several days, one of which seems to have been passed by Rogers, first in chasing his consort for some hours, mistaking her for the Bishop's ship, and then keeping up the joke until she cleared for action, "which I did," he says, "to surprise them." This was a favourite form of practical joke with Rogers, affording no doubt great amusement both to him and his lieutenant, Mr. Frye, when dining together next day "on board the new prize upon a good quarter of mutton and cabbage—a great rarity," adds Rogers, "here."

A week of inaction, however, followed, while the increasing number of the fleet and prisoners, and consequent greater number of mouths to provide for, began to tell rapidly upon their stores, especially of water, "which beginning to grow short, we cannot," says Rogers, "keep the sea much longer." Wherefore, "at a meeting held on board the *Duke*, April 12th, we came to a full resolution to land and attempt Guiaquil." At this meeting it was also decided that the name of that somewhat impetuous sportsman, Mr. Carlton Vanbrugh, should no longer remain on the committee. "He having not only threatened to shoot one of the *Duke's* men at Lobos for refusing to carry some carrion-crows that he shot, but abused Captain Dover."

So long as the ships were at sea, and the work of a purely naval kind, the seamen of the expedition had matters pretty much their own way, and things went on smoothly enough.

But the moment a land expedition was agreed on, disputes quickly arose between Captain Rogers and those of his officers not actually seamen. While speaking of his men, he says, "We know that misfortunes attend sailors put of their element, and hear that they begin to murmur about the encouragement they are to expect for landing;

which they alledge is a risque more than they shipped for."

It was therefore found necessary to come to a definite arrangement as to the disposal of the plunder of Guiaquil before "the mixed gang of most European nations" of which the crews were composed could be induced to enter heartily into an attempt upon it. Rules were, therefore, after much discussion, drawn up for the conduct of all taking part in this little invasion, and "what was to be deemed the men's share" in the booty settled, which included "all manner of bedding and clothes, short of stripping" (whatever that might mean), "gold rings, buckled, buttons, liquors and provisions; with all arms and ammunitions, except great guns for ships;" in a word, everything portable was to be carried off, and be divided equally among the men, the one very honourable exception being "woman's earrings."

It was also settled "that prisoners of note shall be carefully kept as pledges for any of our men that be missing. But that it was desirable no man should trust to this, or be a moment absent from his officers or post." The whole winding up in these words:

> And to prevent all manner of pernicious and mischievous ill-conduct from disorders on shore, we pressingly remind you, that any officer or other that shall be so brutish as to be drunk ashore in an enemie's country, shall not only be severely punished, but lose all share of whatsoever is taken in this expedition. The same punishment to be inflicted on any that disobeys command, or runs from his post, discourages our men, or is cowardly in action, or presumes to burn or destroy anything in the town without our order, or for mischief sake; or that shall be so sneakingly barbarous as to debauch themselves with any prisoners on shore, where we have more generous things to do, both for our own benefit, and the future reputation of ourselves and country. And if all the foregoing rules be strictly followed, we hope to exceed all other attempts of this nature before us in these parts; and not only to enrich ourselves and friends, but even to gain reputation from our enemies. Dated and signed, on board the *Duke* Frigot, the 13th of April, 1709.
>
> Jho. Dover, Pres.
Stephen Courtney.
Woodes Rogers.

The plunder of Guiaquil had scarcely been thus comfortably arranged, and two of the small prizes armed and manned for it, when at daybreak of April the 15th another sail was "sighted between them and the land," and, being calm, both ships' pinnaces were sent in pursuit of her.

Unfortunately, in the hurry of starting for the chase, and expecting little resistance, they neglected to take their swivel guns, or "*patereroes*," with them. The result of which was, that after repeated attempts "to get into a position for boarding, the boats were obliged to retire much dammaged, under a heavy fire of partridge shot and small arms, with the loss of two killed and three wounded: among the former was," says Rogers, "my unfortunate brother, Mr. Thomas Rogers, shot through the head, and instantly died, to my unspeakable sorrow." Philosophically adding, "but as I began this voyage with a resolution to go through it, and the greatest misfortune shall not deter me, I'll as much as possible avoid being thoughtful and afflicting myself for what can't be recalled, but indefatigably pursue the concerns of the voyage, which has hitherto allowed little respite."

The Spanish ship was accordingly followed up and taken that afternoon at 2 p.m., and proved to be the ship from Panama; "but we missed the Bishop," says Rogers, "who ten days before landed at Point St. Helena with his attendants, plate, &c."

After adding another small prize, loaded with *cassia* soap and leather, to the fleet, "on the following day," Rogers says, "about twelve we read the prayers for the dead, and threw my dear brother overboard with one of our sailors; hoisting our colours half mast; and we beginning, the rest of the fleet followed, firing each some volleys of small arms. Our officers expressing great concern for his loss, he being a very hopeful, active young man, a little above twenty years of age."

Even if inclined to do so, Woodes Rogers had now no time for "thoughtfull affliction," his squadron having increased under him from two to eight vessels, with over three hundred prisoners to feed and guard. All which, until his return from the attack upon Guiaquil, were placed on board the frigates and three of the prizes; with orders "to remain at sea forty-eight hours undiscovered, then to sail for Point Arena and anchor there. Irons being put on board every ship because, having many more prisoners than men to guard 'em, we must have 'em well secured."

Two hot days and nights were now passed in the boats of the expedition, rowing and towing their small barks among the islands and mangrove swamps, piloted by Dampier, and one of the Spanish prize captains, up the creeks toward Guiaquil. Great caution being taken to avoid being seen, as "they learnt on landing upon the island of Puna," that a report had been spread among the Spaniards a month before, that they might expect to be "attacked by some English Lords, in seven vessels, from London, under the conduct of an Englishman named Dampier."

Captain Rogers rarely complained of hardships and was not easily frightened, but when lying in his boat under the mangrove bushes, he remarks, "that the muskitoes pestered and stung him grievously; while when at anchor across the tide on a dark night with a small rolling sea, the boat being deep laden and crammed with men," he says, "that though engaged about a charming undertaking he would rather be in a storm at sea than there."

One can hardly help pausing a moment here, to consider the hazardous position of this little body of adventurers, and admire the self-reliance of Rogers and his officers, in venturing upon the sack of Guiaquil, while the small force under them was divided among a fleet of six prizes with 300 prisoners on board to guard and feed. Want of water, as he says, no doubt made some attempt upon the mainland now almost a necessity. Still even this might have been obtained elsewhere; while Rogers' expression, "though engaged upon a charming undertaking," and the building of the launch at Lobos, both point to a preconceived plan having been arranged for this attack, but so timed by him as to appear to the men a mere question of fighting the Spaniards ashore, or perishing at sea for want of water.

It was on the 22nd of April that, after leaving the small *barks* about half way between the island of Puna and the town of Guiaquil, Rogers got with his boats "about 12 at night in sight of the town with no men," but on finding "when abreast of it and ready to land, from abundance of lights, with a confused noise of their bells, a volley of small arms, and two great guns, that the town was alarmed, Captain Dover, the doctor of physick and he fell into a debate of above an hour, as to whether to attack the place then in the dark during this first alarm, or not?" Rogers was of course for pushing on, but Captain Dover and the majority were against him, while Dampier, when asked how the buccaneers would have acted in such a case, said simply enough, "that they never attacked a place after it was once alarmed."

And so, the tide being favourable, the boats dropped down the river again out of sight of the town to the two *barks*; where a further consultation was held among the officers, lying in a boat astern of one of the barks, in order that what was debating might not be overheard by the rest of the company. Which debate ended in Rogers yielding to the majority, and sending two Spanish prisoners to treat with the Correggidore of the town for its ransom, valued by Rogers, with the goods and negroes in his prizes, and "certain new ships then on the stocks near the town," at 40,000 pieces of eight.[1]

As Rogers had foreseen, the Spaniards wisely made use of this time to carry off inland everything of value; and after two days spent in negotiations, made "an offer of 32,000 pieces of eight and no more," upon which, his two *barks* and boats now lying close to the town, he "ordered their interpreter to tell 'em, we had done treating, and after advising all that wished to save their lives to retire out of shot, at once halled down our flag of truce and let fly our English and field colours." And two ship's guns of about six hundred-weight each, mounted on field carriages, being placed in the great launch, Rogers, Captain Dover, and Captain Courtney landed with seventy men from their boats, a lieutenant with others being left on board one of the *barks* to ply her guns over their heads into the town.

"The enemy," says Rogers, "drew up their horse at the end of the street, fronting our men and barks, and lined the houses with men at half musket shot of the bank where we landed, making a formidable show in respect to our little number. We landed and fired every man on his knee at the brink of the bank, then loaded, and as we advanced called to our *bark* to forbear firing, for fear of hurting our men. We who landed kept loading and firing very fast; but the enemy made only one discharge, and retired back to their guns, where their horse drew up a second time. We got to the first houses, and as we opened the street, saw four guns pointing at us before a spacious church, but as our men came in sight firing, the horse scowered off.

"This encouraged me to call to our men to run and seize the guns, and I hastened towards 'em with eight or ten men till within pistol shot, when we all fired, some at the gunners, and others at the men in arms in front of the church, where they were very numerous; but by the time we had loaded and more of our men came in sight, they began to run, and quitted the guns, after firing them with round and partridge, one of the last was discharged at us very near, but, thanks to God, did us no hurt; and they had not time to relade them. By this time the rest of our men were come up with Captain Courtney and Captain Dover, and they, leaving me with a few men to guard the

---

1. A piece of eight was the name then given to the old Spanish dollar, value about four shillings and sixpence.

68

A COUNCIL OF WAR

church, marched to the other end of the town, and so," as Rogers says in his marginal note, "we beat 'em out of the town."

Guards were now posted in all directions round the town, and the Spaniards' guns turned, and left in charge of Captain Dampier to defend the great place in front of the church. While Captain Dover fired some houses that commanded another church in which he had taken up a position, "there being a hill and thick woods near this post, from which the enemy were almost continually popping at him all night." The portable plunder of the town, with the exception "of jars of wine and brandy in great plenty, proved of little value;" while "the sultry, hot, wet unhealthy weather made the carrying of these to the water side a work of great fatigue." Only half-an-hour elapsed from the time of landing until the Spaniards vacated the place, and their loss was but fifteen killed and wounded; while out of Rogers' small force only two were hurt, one of these being "mortally wounded by the bursting of a cohorn shell fired out of one their own mortars on board the *bark*." The following day, Rogers says, "we kept our colours flying on the great church, and sent the Lieutenant of Puna with proposals to ransom the town."

Meanwhile Rogers and his men were busy searching every hole and corner in it for concealed valuables, he having great difficulty while so engaged in preventing his men tearing up "the floor of the great church to look amongst the dead for treasure; but which he would not suffer because of a contagious distemper that had swept off a number of people there not long before, so that this church floor was full of graves." He was himself, however, lucky enough to pick up in this same church "the Corregidore's gold-headed cane," and another with a silver head; "none among the Spaniards," he remarks, "carrying a cane but chief officers, and among them none under a captain wearing a silver or gold-headed one, so that those gentlemen must have been much in haste to leave these badges of office behind them." Besides carrying off "these badges of office," Captain Rogers says, "we unhung a small church bell [2] and sent it aboard for our ships use."

A boat was also sent higher up the river in quest of treasure, and landing, found most of the houses full of women, particularly at one place, where "there were above a dozen handsome genteel young

---

2. In ships of that date the belfry was quite an important, and very ornamental little structure just abaft the forecastle and forard of a space called "No Man's Land," where, between it and the boat on the booms amidships, were stowed all the ropes, blocks, and tackles, likely to be wanted upon the forecastle.

women, well dressed and their hair tied with ribbons very neatly, from whom the men got several gold chains, &c. but were otherwise so civil to them that the ladies offered to dress 'em victuals and brought 'em a cask of good liquor. This," says Rogers, "I mention as a proof of our sailors' modesty, and out of respect to Mr. Connely, and Mr Selkirk, the late Govenour of Juan Fernandez, who commanded this party: for being young men, I was willing to do 'em this justice, hoping the fair sex will make 'em a grateful return when we arrive in Great-Britain on account of their civil behaviour to these charming prisoners."

Besides this pleasing account of their treatment of, and by, the Spanish ladies, these modest young officers "brought back with them gold chain, plate, &c., to the value of over £1000, and reported, that in places above the town they saw several parties of more than 300 armed Horse and foot, so that we apprehend," says Rogers, "the enemy designe to gain time by pretending to pay ransom, till, with vast odds, they may attack us and reckon themselves sure of victory."

After many alarms by night, and much skirmishing by day, in which Rogers lost two more men, the prisoners on the 26th of April returned with an offer of 30,000 pieces of eight for the town, ships, and barks, to be paid in twelve days. "Which time Rogers did not approve of," and sent his final answer to the effect that "they would see the town all on fire by three that afternoon, unless they agreed to give sufficient hostages for the money to be paid within six days." Upon which, about 1 p.m., the prisoners came back with two men on horseback, the required hostages, and said their terms were accepted; and the Spanish agreement arrived the following morning "sighned by 'em," an English one being sent in return as follows to them:

Whereas the City of Guiaquil, lately in *subjection* to Philip. V. King of Spain, is now taken by storm, and in the possession of Captains Thomas Dover, Woodes Rogers, and Stephen Courtney, Commanding a body of Her Majesty of Great Britain's subjects: We the underwritten are content to become hostages for the said city, and to continue in the custody of the said Captains till 30,000 pieces of eight shall be paid to them for the ransom of the said city, two new ships, and six *barks*; the said sum to be paid at Puna in six days from the date hereof; During which time no hostility is to be committed on either side between this and Puna; After payment the hostages to be discharged, and all prisoners to be delivered up; otherwise the said hostages do agree to remain prisoners till the said sum is discharged in any other part of the world. In witness whereof we have voluntarily set our hands, this 27th day of April Old Stile and the 7th of May N.S. in the year of our Lord 1709.

Which remarkable document was signed by the two hostages, "who, with all the things we have got together were shipped off," says Rogers, "by 11 o'clock the same morning; after which, with our colours flying, we marched through the town to our *barks*; when I, marching in the rear with a few men, picked up several pistols, cutlashes, and poleaxes; which shewed that our men were grown very careless, weak and weary of being soldiers, and that 'twas time to be gone from hence."

On the whole Rogers seems to have thought that the Spaniards got the better of him in this bargain. "For though upon weighing anchor at 8 next morning from Guiaquil," he says, "we made what shew and noise we could with our drums, trumpets, and guns, and thus took leave of the Spaniards very cheerfully;" he ends with the remark, "though not half so well pleased as we should have been had we taken 'em by surprise. For I was well assured from all hands that at least we should then have got above 200,000 pieces of eight in money, and a greater plenty of such necessaries as we now found.

"Among which was about 250 bags of flower, beans, peas, and rice, 15 jars of oil, about 160 jars of other liquors, some cordage, ironware and small nails, with four jars of powder, a tun of pitch and tar, a parcel of clothing and necessaries, and as I guess," says Rogers, "about £1200 in plate, earings *et cetera*, and 150 bales of dry goods, 4 guns, and 200 Spanish ordinary useless arms and musket barrels, a few packs of indigo, cocoa, and *anotto*, with about a tun of loaf sugar. Besides these which we took, we left abundance of goods in the town, with liquors of most sorts, sea stores several warehouses full of cocoa, divers ships on the stocks, and two new ships unrigged upwards of 400 tuns, which cost 80,000 crowns and lay at anchor before the town. And by which it appears the Spaniards had a good bargain; but a ransom for these things was far better for us than to burn what we could not carry off.

"Among the casualties that occurred to the men during the occupation of Guiaquil," Rogers says, "a French man belonging to my company, sent with others to strengthen Captain Courteney's quarters, being put centinel, shot Hugh Tidcomb one of our men, so that he died. This accident happening by a two severe order to shoot any in the night that did not answer, neither this man nor the centinel understanding how to ask or answer the watchword. By which neglect a man was unaccountably lost."

While of those wounded in the confusion of a night attack "was a man shot against the middle of his pole axe [3] that hung at his side, which shot made an impression on the iron and bruised the part under it, so that it proved a piece of armour well placed." Captain Courteney's chief lieutenant was also wounded upon the outside of the thickest part of his leg by one of his pistols hanging at his side, which unluckily discharged itself, leaving a bullet in the flesh, but with little danger to his life. Which incidents kept all on the alert at night, "the centinels calling to each other every quarter of an hour to prevent 'em sleeping."

No doubt the men that took an active part in this attempt upon Guiaquil were the pick of the frigates' crews. But it speaks well for their state of discipline that only one, "a Dutchman, so much as transgressed orders by drinking beyond his bearing," and he, after being missed for a day or two, came aboard before they sailed, having been roused "out of his brandy-wine-fit, and his arms restored to him by the honest man of the house where he lay."

The pleasing relations between Captain Rogers and his Guiaquil prisoners and hostages were quite remarkable about this time, and he mentions more than one little act of courtesy towards them; among others that, "on parting with the Lieutenant of Puna, he gave him four old sick negroes, and a damaged bail of goods for what we had taken from him, being a man we had some respect for; and that he also parted very friendly with several of our prisoners we took at sea, particularly an old *padre* that I had treated civilly at my own table ever since we took him, for which he was extremely thankful."

In his description of the "Province of Guiaquil, for the information of such as have not been in those parts," Rogers gives a table of "ten sorts of men besides Spaniards there;" *viz.*, "the Mustees, Fino Mustees, Terceroons de Indies, Quateroons de Indies, Mullattoes, Quateroons de Negroes, Terceroons de Negroes, Indians, Negroes, and Sambos;" but adds, "that though these be the common sorts, they have rung the

---

3. Pole axe, a hatchet like a battle axe, with a short handle, and furnished with a sharp point at the back of its head. Used chiefly to cut away the rigging of an enemy attempting to board. It is also employed in boarding an enemy whose hull is more lofty than the boarder's, by driving the points of several axes into the enemy's ship's side, thereby forming a sort of scaling-ladder; hence it is often called a boarding-axe.

changes so often upon these peals of generations that there is no end of their distinctions, so that the King of Spain is here able to match the skins of his *Americans* to any colour, with more variety and exactness than a draper can match his cloth and trimming."

The accounts given of Guiaquil by the "French Buccaneers *alias* pirates are," he says; "very false, though they left their infamous mark, of having been there about twenty-two years ago, when in their attack on the place they lost a great many men, and afterwards committed a great deal of brutishness and murther."

Though Woodes Rogers himself would now rank little above a pious sort of pirate, it is curious to note from what he says here, and again after visiting the Gallapagos Islands, one of the chief haunts of the buccaneers, that he looked upon then as much below him socially, while after his own experience in these seas, he evidently mistrusted the accounts of their exploits there as exaggerated or romantic tales of little value to future navigators.

It was on their way "towards these Gallapagos islands," piloted no doubt by Dampier, that on the 11th of May seventy men in the *Duke* and *Dutchess* fell ill of a malignant fever, which, from its attacking only those engaged in the late operations at Guiaquil, was most likely contracted there by them.

Among those taken ill was "Captain Courtney. Captain Dover going on board the *Dutchess* to prescribe for him." While on the 15th Mr. Hopkins, Dr. Dover's kinsman and assistant, died on board the *Duke*, "being," says Rogers, "a very good-tempered sober man well beloved by the whole ship's company, having read prayers for us once a day ever since we passed the Equinox."

A day seldom passed now without a record by Rogers of the death of one or two of the best of his crew, there being sixty sick men on board the *Duke*, and eighty in the *Dutchess* at one time; and though there was no want of doctors in either ship, the store of medicines began to run very short. So that, thinking prevention better than cure, "and finding punch preserve my own health, I did at this time," says Rogers, "prescribe it freely among such of our company as were well, to preserve theirs."

The Gallapagos, when found, were searched one after the other in vain for fresh water, until, after getting a few turtle and some fish there, the number of sick, and want of water, compelled them to steer for the island of Gorgona, near the mainland.

CHAPTER 5

Among the Gallapagos Islands and at Gorgona Road in Peru

While engaged cruising among the Gallapagos, two more small prizes were however added to the fleet, but, at the same time, great anxiety was felt as to the safety of one of the recent prizes, a small *bark* under the command of a Mr. Hatley, which was lost sight of here, with only two days' water on board. And after several days of unsuccessful search she was "bewailed as lost," it being supposed that Hatley and his prize crew of three men had been surprised and overpowered while asleep by the two Spaniards and three negro prisoners on board her.[1]

Besides careening the frigates and landing their sick men while in Gorgona Road, arrangements were made with certain Spaniards of note among the prisoners for the purchase, or rather what Rogers called the ransom, of the large gallion-built ship, with the other small prizes and their cargoes; but the stout French-built ship, the *Havre de Grace*, in attempting the capture of which Rogers' brother was killed, was not sold, but after being re-christened the *Marquiss*, was re-fitted, and armed with nine guns, as an additional cruiser.

It was in discharging cargo before careening her, that "500 bales of Pope's bulls were found, which, taking up abundance of room in the

---

1. On returning to England, Rogers learnt that Mr. Hatley's *bark* was not lost; but that, after pluckily keeping the sea for a fortnight without water, he was forced to make for the mainland; where he and his companions fell into the hands of some Spanish Indians, and were by them tied up to a tree, whipped, and otherwise illtreated, their lives being only saved by a *padre*, who interfered and cut them down; after which Hatley remained a prisoner at Lima for some time. After his return to England, Hatley, some years later, accompanied Captain Shelvolke on his unfortunate voyage round the world; and it is said that the "Albatross" incident in the *Ancient Mariner* was suggested by one recorded in that voyage.

ship, we throwed overboard," says Rogers, "to make room for better goods, except what we used to burn the pitch off our ship's bottoms when we careened 'em." These bulls or indulgences, he says, "though they cannot be read, the print looking worse than any of our old ballads, are sold here by the clergy for 3 *ryals* to 50 pieces of eight each."

Though Rogers rarely lets a chance pass of having a shot at the Pope, he was far from having bigoted or puritanical ideas about the Catholic religion, for in speaking of his treatment of some of his prisoners of the better class, he says, "We allowed liberty of conscience on board our floating commonwealth, and there being a priest in each ship, they had the great cabin for their Mass, whilst we used the Church of England service over them on the quarter deck; so that the papists here were the Low Church men."

Other reasons, not connected with his prisoners' liberty of conscience, may have had something to do with this arrangement. It happened, however, curiously enough, that about this time Rogers and his crew, quite unintentionally, assisted in the making of what afterwards became, no doubt, a very valuable relique to the Romanists here. For while discharging the cargo of the Spanish gallion-built ship, he says, "A large wooden effigy of the Virgin Mary was either dropt or thrown overboard, which drove ashoar near the north point of the island, from whence some Indians there a-fishing, brought her in their canoe to the shoar over against our ship, where we gave our prisoners liberty to walk that day. Who, as soon as they saw her, crossed and blessed themselves, and fancied this must be the Virgin come by water from Lima to help them, and set the image up on shoar and wiped it dry with cotton, and when they come aboard told us, that though they had wiped her again and again, she continued to sweat very much; while all those around were devoutly amazed, praying and telling their beads. They shewed this cotton to the ransomers and the interpreter wet by the excessive sweat of the Holy Virgin, which they kept as a choice relick."

"Before this," says Rogers, "when I heard the like stories, I took 'em to have been invented meerly to ridicule the Romanists; but when I found such silly stories believed by eight grave men of a handsome appearance and good reputation amongst the Spaniards, I was convinced of the ignorance and credulity of the Papists."

Just after the valuation and sale of the plunder of Guiaquil and the prizes was settled, a mutiny was discovered among the crew of the *Duke*, sixty of whom signed a paper, expressing discontent at the large share of plunder assigned to "the gentlemen that were officers, though not sailors, amongst us." But a little firmness, combined with a judicious use of the bilboes on Rogers' part, with an abatement on three of these gentlemen's shares, soon brought his men to reason; "while though," says Rogers, "sailors usually exceed all measures when left to themselves on these occasions, I must own ours have been more obedient than any ship's crew engaged in a like undertaking I ever heard of;" adding, "but if any sea officer thinks himself endowed with patience and industry, let him command a privateer and descharge his office well in a distant voyage, and I'll engage he shall not want opportunities to improve, if not to exhaust, all his stock."

It must be remembered that Captain Rogers wrote this little growl, and found his stock of patience running short, on the equator, in a small ship, half full of sick men, and soon after what he calls "those general misunderstandings, and several unhappy differences among us, arrising out of, and before our attack on Guiaquil." That Rogers had at this time even more difficult questions and people to deal with, is shown by an entry in his log, that, "amongst the prisoners taken on board the last prize from Panama was a gentlewoman and her family, her eldest daughter, a pretty young woman of about 18 newly married, and her husband with her, to whom we assigned the great cabin of the prize, none being suffered to intrude amongst them.

"Yet I was told the husband shewed evident marks of jealously, the Spanish's epidemick, but I hope he had not the least reason for it amongst us, my third lieutenant, Glendall, alone having charge of the ship, who being above 50 years of age appeared to us the most secure guardian to females that had the least charm;" which is followed by the description of "an ugly creature called by the Spaniards a sloth, caught in Gorgona, and which," says Rogers, "being let go at the lower part of the mizen shrouds was two hours getting to the masthead, keeping all the time an equal and slow pace as if he walked by art and all his movements had been directed by clockwork within him."

"Many monkeys were shot in Gorgona Island, *fricassees* and broth being made of them for the sick men." But though "Captain Dampier, who had been accustomed to such food, said he never eat anything in London that seemed so delicious as a monkey or baboon of these parts, none of the *Duke's* officers would touch them, provisions being not yet scarce enough." Rogers also describes the "land turtles *alias* tortoises caught in the Gallapagos islands as the ugliest creatures in nature, with a shell black as jet not unlike the top of an old hackney coach; the neck long, about the bigness of a man's wrist, with club feet as big as ones fist, shaped like those of an elephant, the head little and visage small like a snake, looking very very old and black." He adds: "they lay eggs on our deck about the size of gooses, white with a large thick shell exactly round."

After leaving Gorgona, the *Duke*, *Dutchess*, and *Marquiss*, on the 25th of August, bore away for Tecames Road, in order to trade with the natives and Spaniards there for fresh provisions, &c. The Indians here, however, were at first disposed to fight rather than trade, so that while careening the ships half the men had to be kept under arms; until Rogers happily thought of conciliating them with "a present of three large wooden Spanish saints he had on board, and which, with a feathered cap for the chiefs wife," were sent on shore. Besides these "wooden saints," a portion of the prize goods on board the *Duke* consisted of about thirty-five negroes, and these not being readily turned into money at this time, were, "being lusty fellows," mustered by Rogers, and, "after taking the names of those that had any, and giving names to those that wanted them, were placed with arms and powder in charge of Michael Kendall, a free negro of Jamaica who deserted from the Spaniards at Gorgona, with orders to drill them continually to act as marines in case we meet an enemy."

While, in order to encourage, and make this black contingent as presentable as possible, "they were given bays" (baize) "for clothing, and with a dram all round to confirm the contract, were told that now they must look upon themselves as Englishmen, and no more as negro slaves to the Spaniards." With which rough and ready form of emancipation and British baptism, "they," says Rogers, "expressed themselves highly pleased; while I promise myself good assistance from them, bearing in mind the proverb, that those who know nothing of danger, fear none;" while in order to further perfect these negroes and the men in the use of the great guns and small arms, the *Dutchess*, at ten one morning, hoisted Spanish colours, and a sham fight was arranged, "during which everyone acted the part he ought have done if in earnest, firing with ball excepted.

"Our prisoners were secured in the hold with the surgeons, and to imitate the business for them, I ordered," says Rogers, "red lead mixed with water to be thrown upon two of our fellows and sent 'em down to the surgeons, who were much surprised, and thinking they had been really wounded, went about to dress them, but finding their mistake, it was a very agreable diversion."

"Here to I must not forget," says Rogers, "a Welchman that told me he took the ship we were going to engage for the *Dutchess*, till he saw the Spanish colours, and that being overjoyed with the hopes of a good prize he loaded his musket with shot, and designed to fire among the thickest part of 'em, which he would certainly have done had he not been forbid. By which it appears that blundering fools may have courage."

On the afternoon of Nov. 4th, "the *Dutchess* being near, Rogers sent his yawl aboard with Lieutenant Glendall, to agree exactly on some remarkable land, that each of us knowing the same landmark, might the better keep our stations. We agreed also that the *Marquiss* should now be in the middle with the *Dutchess* next the shore." Two days later it was arranged between the captains of the *Duke* and *Dutchess* that the outer berth should be exchanged for the inner one every two days, in order, says Rogers, "that we may have equal chances for seeing the Manila ship, because I now think the inner birth the likeliest; Sir Thomas Cavendish in Queen Elizabeth's time having took the Spanish galleon in this place on the 4th of November."

An old salt, in the days when yachting was almost unknown, used to say, "that a man who went to sea for pleasure, would be likely to go to hell for pastime." Englishmen and Americans, however, do now go to sea not only for amusement, but spend large sums in doing so, many of these being men who, in Rogers' time, would no doubt have gone to sea for gain, and the pleasure and excitement of Spanish galleon-hunting. But three weary months, like those now spent in the *Duke* and *Dutchess*, cruising under a tropical sun off Cape St. Lucas, waiting and watching for the "Manila ship," were enough to try the patience of the most ardent of galleon-hunters.

It is not surprising, therefore, that a sea parliament had at this time to assemble on board the *Duke* to pass measures for the prevention and punishment of gambling, which had so increased of late among the officers and crews of the ships, that some of the men had lost the greater part of their share in the plunder recently divided among them. It was probably one of these reckless gamblers that was ordered into irons about this time "for wishing himself a pirate, or that an enemy was alongside who could overpower us"—a wish which must have appeared even more atrocious to Captain Rogers than did that of Mr. Squeers' pupil, "the juniorest Palmer," who after first "wishing he was in heaven," went on to "wish he was a donkey, because then he wouldn't have a father as didn't love him!"

Among the measures passed "against wagering and gaming" on board the frigates, the most useful was one repudiating "all debts contracted from man to man, unless attested by the commanders and entered on the ship's books;" which strange old-motherly resolution was "agreed to and signed by the officers and men in each ship in sight of California, Nov. 11th, 1709."

The tedium of this long cruise was broken once by touching at the islands of Tres Marias for wood and water, and again by a second visit to the Galapagos in hopes of falling in with "poor Hatley and his *bark*;" but nothing was found there beyond some traces of the buccaneers in the shape of wreckage and broken wine jars. Rogers also mentions at this time, as an event of some importance, the birth on board the *Duke* of "a tawny coloured negro girl," the mother being a negress from Guiaquil, kept among other prize goods of the same class to act as laundresses,[2] and seamstresses on board the ships.

Both mother and child were well cared for, a close cabin being provided for her, together with a "bottle of thick strong Peru wine." This interesting event was evidently not looked upon by Captain Rogers as an unmixed blessing, for he says that "he gave our other she-negro nymph (called Daphne) strict orders to be careful not to transgress in this way."

Provisions of all sorts, especially bread, were, "after a strick rummage of the ships," now found to be running short, while their new consort, the *Marquiss*, was discovered to be defective and leaking, and had to be taken to the "port of Segura," for repairs. "So that," Rogers says, "we all looked very melancholy, necessity compelling us to no longer continue cruising for the Manila ship, but sail at once across the Pacific for the island of Guam in order to revictual before starting for China and the Indies, and thence round the Cape of Good Hope, for England."

This was, however, scarcely decided upon, when, on December 21st, at nine a.m., a man "at the mast head cried out he saw another sail as well as the *Dutchess*," which, though at first thought to be the *Marquiss* rejoining them, proved "after several wagers" to be the

---

2. Even in Nelson's time, and later, it was not unusual to find women, the wives of petty officers, on board a man-of-war in commission, who acted as washerwomen, and helped the surgeons and their mates in the sick-bay, or on the orlop deck among the wounded in time of action; and the author can remember one of these old ladies, about forty years ago, living in the island of Jersey with her husband, a retired gunner, who had been in the actions of the Nile and Trafalgar.

long expected "Acapulco ship." The weather continued calm that day, which "kept them all in a very uncertain languishing condition," and the chase had to be tended during the night by "two pinnaces showing false fires, that we might know whereabouts they and the chase was."

But a little after daybreak on the 23rd, still having no wind, Rogers says, "we *got* out *eight* of our *ship's oars*, and rowed above an hour, when there sprung up a small breeze, upon which I ordered a large kettle of chocolate to be made for our ship's company, (having no spiritous liquor to give them) and then went to prayers, but before we had concluded, were disturbed by the enemy firing at us. She had barrels hanging at each yard arm, which looked like powder barrels to deter us from boarding. The *Dutchess* being to leeward, with little wind, did not come up. And the enemy firing her stern chase several times, we returned it with our forechase, till getting close aboard, we gave her several broadsides, plying our small arms briskly, which they returned as thick for awhile, but did not ply their guns so fast as we.

"After a little while shooting ahead of them we lay athawt their hawse close aboard, and plyed them so warmly, that she soon struck her colours two-thirds down; and the *Dutchess* coming up, fired five guns and a volley of small shot, to which she made no reply, having submitted. This Galleon was," says Rogers, "called by the long name of *Nostra Signiora de la Incarnacion Desengàno*, Sir John Pichberty, Commander, she had twenty guns, with twenty *patereroes* and 193 men, whereof nine were killed, ten wounded, and several blown up and burnt with powder.

"We engaged them about three glasses" (an hour and a half), "in which time we had only myself and another wounded. I being shot through the left cheek, the bullet striking away great part of my upper jaw, and several teeth which dropt down on the deck where I fell. The other was an Irish landman slightly wounded. A shot disabled our mizenmast, and I was forced to write what I would say to prevent the loss of blood, and because of the pain I suffered by speaking."

On examining the officers on board the prize, they learnt that "she left Manila in company with a much larger vessel; but having lost sight of her about three months ago, they thought she must be got to Acapulco before now. The latter part of this information was evidently not relied on, for measures were at once taken to secure and leave the present prize and prisoners at Port Segura, and start the *Dutchess* with the *Marquiss*," which they found in "sailing posture there," on an eight days' cruise for the other galleon, the *Nostra Seniora del Incarnacion Dessengàno*, now re-christened the *Batchelor*, to remain in port with as many men as could be spared to guard and refit her.

"Her sails being removed, and the prisoners, of whom there were 170, secured for the time on board a small *bark*, anchored a mile distant from her without her rudder, sails, or boat, with a few men to give them victuals and drink. Rogers' wound must have been serious, for on the 24th he says, "In the night I felt something clog my throat, which I swallowed with much pain, and suppose it was a part of my jaw bone or the shot, which we can't yet give account of;" adding, "but I soon recovered myself, only my throat and head being greatly swelled, I have much ado to swallow any sorts of liquid for sustenance," which made him very weak; and, what was worse, "that he spoke in great pain, and not loud enough to be heard at any distance."

But though the surgeons and chief officers wished him to stay in port on board the prize, he was unable to resist the temptation, when, on the afternoon of the 26th, "two sentries who had been placed upon a hill above the port signalled by three waffs that a third sail was in sight, as well as the *Dutchess* and *Marquiss*," of joining his consorts as soon as possible, in command of his own ship. Captain Dover remaining on board the prize.

It was 7 p.m., and soon quite dark, before the *Duke* was under weigh; but at daybreak next morning all three vessels were sighted to windward, distant about four leagues; the wind remained scant, however, all day, so that Rogers and his crew had the mortification of seeing first the *Marquiss* and then the *Dutchess* briskly engage the galleon without being able to join them; in fact it was midnight before they did so, and then only to find that the *Marquiss* had fired away nearly all her powder and shot with little or no effect, her guns being too small, and that of the *Dutchess* had been forced to stretch away, with several men wounded, from the Spaniard, to repair her foremast and other defects, among which was a shot in her powder-room.

"Curiously enough," Rogers says, "the Spaniard had been making signals to the *Duke*, and edging towards her all day, mistaking her for her lost consort, until just before dusk, otherwise, having little wind, and that against us, we should not have been up with her at all." The following day, however, the *Duke* was near enough to join in the fight, but only to find, as the *Dutchess* and *Marquiss* had done before her, that their largest shot (six-pounders) did very little hurt to the galleon, a brave new ship, the *Bignonia*, of 900 tons and 60 guns, and well provided with close-quarters,[3] and her waist protected by strong board-ing-netting.[4] The *Dutchess* had now twenty men killed and wounded, while a fire-ball from the enemy's round-top, lighting on the *Duke's* quarter-deck, blew up an ammunition chest, by which Mr. Vanbrugh and a Dutchman were much burnt; while Rogers says, "Just before we blew up on the quarter deck I was unfortunately wounded by a splinter in the left foot, part of my heel bone being struck out and ankle cut above half through, which bled very much before it could be dressed, and weakened me so that I could not stand, but lay on my back in great misery." From first to last they had been engaged six or seven hours, and placed not less than 500 shot in the galleon; yet there she lay "driving," the Spanish flag obstinately flying from her maintop-mast head, "all our battering signifying little beyond killing two men in her tops, and shattering her rigging."

As all this fighting was simply of a commercial character, a coun-cil was now assembled on board the *Duke*, and though the Spaniard still "lay with his mainyard aback, expecting another brush," it was at once decided, "that after keeping the galleon company till night, they should then lose her, and return to the harbour to look after the prize already taken." This measure was the more urgent as ammunition of all sorts was running short, and the *Duke's* mainmast shot through miser-ably in two places, so that it settled to it, threatening every moment to fall by the board, and bring other spars down with it; which, as they had a long voyage before them, and masts not easily got there without great delay, might even endanger the safety of the whole expedition.

It was indeed lucky for them that they did not attempt to board this great ship, for they learnt afterwards that her complement of men amounted to 450, besides passengers; while in all three ships they had now less than 120 men left fit for boarding. Soon after this the "Span-iard filled her sails and made away W.N.W.," glad enough, no doubt, to lose sight of them, though in size and force she was quite equal to the great galleon that, to Lord Anson's surprise, bore down upon the

---

3. "Close-quarters." Strong barriers of wood across a ship in certain places, used as a retreat when boarded, fitted with loop-holes for small arms, and often with powder-chests on the deck over them, which can be fired from the close-quarters upon a boarding party.

4. Boarding-nettings extended fore and aft above the gunwale to a proper height up the rigging, to prevent an enemy jumping aboard.

Anson says that, in addition to these, the galleon taken by him "was provided against boarding both by 'close-quarters,' and a strong net of two-inch rope laced over her waist, defended by half pikes."

The Duke takes the Manila ship

Centurion, of 60 guns, instead of trying to avoid her. Weight of metal, however, enabled him to make as short work of that galleon as Rogers did of the smaller one.

Rogers himself, however, was of opinion that had the *Duke* and *Dutchess* attacked this ship together in the first instance, they would have taken her, and was most anxious for that reason that the *Dutchess* and *Marquiss* should not go out of port until his ship was ready to sail. The majority, however, decided then that he should remain in port until the arrangements for the security of the smaller galleon and her prisoners were completed. Upon arriving at Port Segura the prisoners, with Captain Pichberty, his officers, and a *padre*, were supplied with water and provisions, and after acknowledging in writing "that they had been very civilly treated," were despatched in the small *bark* to Acapulco.

CHAPTER 6

Sailing Round the Cape of Good Hope, Home

Before sailing for Guam, it was necessary to appoint a commander for their new consort, the *Batchelor* frigate, and Captain Dover having, it seems, a large money-stake in the ships, was, much against Rogers' wish, selected by the majority for this post. But under protest from Rogers, who as he lay, no doubt in great misery, on his back, recounts "how it was now after taking this rich prize our great misfortune to have a paper war amongst ourselves." Rogers' chief objection to Captain Dover was "that owing to his violent temper, capable men could not well act under him, while as a Dr of physick he was incapable as a seaman himself."

A peace was, however, patched up by appointing Mr. Robert Prye, Rogers' first lieutenant, and Mr. William Stretton to take sole charge of the ship as to navigation, with Mr. Selkirk and another as chief mates; Captain Dover to have command in other matters.

And being a large ship, "thirty good men were sent on board her from the *Duke*, with twenty-five from the *Dutchess*, and thirteen from the *Marquiss*, which, with thirty-six Manila Indians, called *Lascarrs*, and other prisoners will," says Rogers, "bring up her complement to 110 men."

Before sailing, "ten of the *Duke's* guns were struck down into the hold, to ease the ship, being altogether useless betwixt here and the East Indies."

The voyage from Cape St. Lucas in California to Guam, one of the Ladrone islands, occupied fifty-eight days, the best day's run being 168 miles, and the worst 41. The distance sailed by reckoning was 6,300 miles, which gives an average of 108 miles a day, about equal to a speed of four and a half miles an hour, which may "seem slow to us,[1] but it must be remembered that the speed of the dullest sailer was that of all the others in company; and that besides the loss of speed due to the rapid fouling of uncoppered ships in the tropics, it was the custom then to shorten sail after dark.

Beyond the death of many wounded men, and the burial of "a negro named Depford, who being very much addicted to stealing of provisions, his room was more acceptable at this time than his company," nothing of importance is recorded after leaving Port Segura on the 11th of January until the 14th of February, when, "in commemoration of the ancient custom, of chusing valentines," Rogers "drew up a list of the fair ladies in Bristol that were in any ways related to or concerned in the ships, and sent for his officers into the cabin, where everyone drew and drank a ladies health in a cup of punch, and to a happy sight of 'em all, which I did," he says, "to put 'em in mind of home."

The *Duke* had been leaky for some time, and after many attempts to stop the leak with bonnet-pieces, &c., one pump had to be constantly kept going, two men of each watch taking an hour's spell at the pump at a time; "which labour, together with being on short allowance," Rogers says, "makes our people look miserably." So that there was much rejoicing among all hands at sighting Guam on March the 11th; but though "several flying *prows* came off to look at the ships, and run by them very swift," none could be tempted to venture aboard until Rogers hoisted Spanish colours, when "on turning into the harbour one came under his stern with two Spaniards in her, who being told in Spanish, in answer to their questions, that they were friends from New Spain, willingly came on board, and enquired whether they had any letters for the Govenour? We had one ready," says Rogers, "and detaining one Spaniard on board, sent the other ashore with our letter, which was thus.

"We, being servants of Her Majesty of Great Britain, stopping at these islands on our way to the East Indies, will not molest the settlement provided you deal friendly with us, being willing to pay for whatever provisions you can spare, &c. But, if after this civil request, you do not act like a man of honour, and deny us our request, you may immediately expect such military treatment as we are with ease able to give you.

---

1. The speed of Rogers' little squadron across the Pacific, under sail, was barely half that of the British Fleet which in July, 1888, was able to make the passage under steam from Portsmouth to Bantry Bay, Ireland, at a mean speed of eight knots!

Signed, Woodes Rogers, S. Courtney, and E. Cooke."

This letter appears to have acted like a charm upon the Governor of Guam and his officers, for he at once answered "with a present of four bullocks, one for each ship, with limes oranges and cocoanuts. And being now arrived," says Rogers, "at a place of peace and plenty, we all became indifferent well reconciled among ourselves after the misunderstandings at California which had been so much increased of late by our shortness of water and provisions."

And in return for the Governor's civility, an entertainment was "provided for him and four Spanish gentlemen on board the *Bachelor*, where we all met, and made 'em," says Rogers, "as welcome as time and place would afford, with musick and our sailors dancing, when I, not being able to move myself, was hoisted in a chair out of my ship and the boat into the *Batchelor*."

Considering that he was in an enemy's port. Captain Rogers appears to have rapidly established diplomatic relations with the Governor of Guam of a most friendly and agreeable kind. For this entertainment was followed by one of the same sort on board the *Duke*, *Dutchess*, and *Marquiss*, which were returned by the Governor and his suite on shore; when Rogers and his brother officers, after partaking of "sixty dishes of various sorts," presented the Governor, in return for his four bullocks and civility, with "two negro boys dressed in liveries together with scarlet clothe serge and six peeces of cambric."

And after purchasing "14 small lean cattel, two cows and calves, 60 hogs, 100 fowls, with Indian corn, rice, yams and cocoa nuts" in proportion, Rogers ended his week's stay at the island by leaving there an old Spaniard "called Antonio Gomes Figuero, whom they took in the first prize in the South seas, designing to carry him to Great Britain," as a witness upon any question which might arise there respecting other prizes taken in the South Seas.

"But he, being in all appearance not likely to live, we dismissed him here; he first giving a certificate that he saw us take certain *barks* and prisoners subjects to Philip V. King of Spain." Rogers was so pleased as a seaman with the speed and handiness of the flying *proahs* of Guam (or as he spells it, "*prows*")—which, he says, "by what I saw, I believe may run twenty miles an hour, for they passed our ships like a bird flying"—that he carried one of them with him to London, thinking it might be worth fitting up there as a curiosity on the canal in St. James's Park. This was more than thirty years before the account of these "flying *proahs*" appeared in Anson's, voyage.

The *Duke* continued so leaky at this time, that before leaving Guam Rogers decided upon handing over to Captain Courtney a chest of plate and money to be put on board the *Dutchess*. While Rogers himself "being still very weak and not able to stand," it was agreed that Captain Courtngy, in the *Dutchess*, should lead the squadron by night through the almost unknown straits of Molucca, and among the various reefs, shoals, and islands they must pass in the passage to the island of Bouton or Boutong, where they designed to wood and water on their way to Batavia.

The order of sailing was therefore "for the *Dutchess* to keep ahead with a light, her pinnace when possible to be ahead of her, all signals for tacking or altering course to be given by the *Dutchess*." So little was this part of the world then known to the English, that even Dampier, their pilot, who had been there twice, and was the discoverer of some of these islands in 1699, seems to have lost his way; so that they were glad to get hold of the Malay skipper of a small native *bark*, and persuade him by bribes, in spite of his fear of the Dutch, to act as pilot between Bouton and Batavia. Rogers says, however, that "this way into India would not be difficult if better known."

After leaving Guam the weather was for some days dark, squally, and unsettled, with thunder and lightning, and mention is made of more than one ugly gale of wind, while three tropical April showers, in the form of water-spouts, were met with on the 15th of that month, one of which had like to have broke on the *Marquiss* had not the *Dutchess* broke it before it reached her, by firing two shots.

The horrid apparition still draws nigh,
And white with foam the whirling billows fly,
The guns were primed; the vessel northward veers.
Till her black battery on the column bears:
The nitre fired: and, while the dreadful sound
Convulsive shook the slumbering air around.
The watery volume, trembling to the sky.
Burst down a dreadful deluge from on high!

Falconer.

On the 29th of May, however, the four ships were safely anchored at the island of Bouton; but stayed there only long enough to water and get a supply of fresh fruit and vegetables; Rogers finding the king of the island both "dilatory and designing in his dealings with them," notwithstanding which, before sailing, they made him "a present of a

Bishop's cap, a thing of little use to us, but what he highly esteemed and gratefully accepted of."

It was on the 17th of June, 1710, near the north coast of Java, that the *Duke* and *Dutchess* met the first vessel bound east from Europe since they sailed from Bristol in August, 1708. She was a Dutch ship of 600 tons and 50 guns, from whom they learnt "that Queen Anne's Consort, Prince George of Denmark, was dead. That the wars continued in Europe, where we had good success in Flanders, but little elsewhere."

And what was of more importance to them at that time than any European news, they "borrowed" from this ship, "a large draft of those parts."

In addition to the troubles of a leaky ship, with the clank of her pump constantly ringing in his ear, and the dangers of an intricate navigation among coral reefs, &c., Rogers tells us that here "their voyage was like to have been ruined by the mutinous conduct of an officer on board his ship, with other officers and men on board the *Dutchess* which knot was only broken by putting the *leaders* in irons," &c.

On anchoring in Batavia Road, however, matters smoothed down rapidly, at least so far as the men were concerned, for Rogers says, "'Till now I find that I was a stranger to the humours of our ship's company some of whom are hugging each other, while others bless themselves that they were come to such a glorious place for punch, where *arack* is eightpence per gallon, and sugar one penny a pound, whereas a few weeks past a bowl of punch to them was worth half the voyage."

While personally Captain Rogers is made happy, and congratulates himself, first, "on the discovery of a large musket shot, which the doctor now cut out of his mouth, it having been there six months, so that the upper and lower jaw being broken and almost closed, he had much ado to come at it;" and next, "that several pieces of his foot and heel bone having been removed, he believes himself, thank God, in a fair way to have the use of his foot and recover his health."

Though Rogers makes light of these trifling operations and discomforts, and they are not pleasant subjects to dwell on, they could not be passed without notice, as pointing out distinctly the sort of man physically fit to have charge of "a charming undertaking" of this kind, while considering the ways of life on ship-board in those days, and the climate he was in at this time, the marvel is not that "he now thought himself in a fair way to recover his health," but that he lived

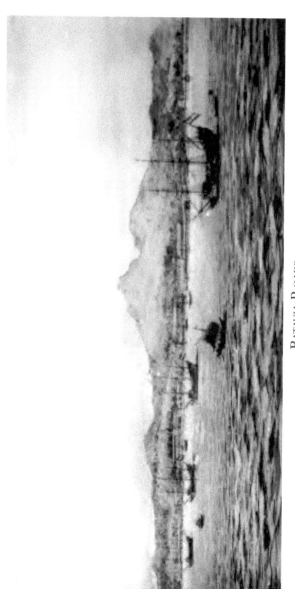

BATAVIA ROADS

to reach home and write his travels.[2]

They anchored in Batavia Roads on the 20th of June, where they found "betwixt thirty and forty sail great and small," and having, "as customary," says Rogers, "lost almost a day in running so far west round the globe, we here altered our account of time."

A complete overhaul, both of ships and prize goods, was now made; and all bale goods carefully repacked in "waxcloth, and tarpaulins."

While the *Marquiss*, being found much honeycombed by the worm, was condemned as unfit for the voyage home "about the Cape of Good Hope," and after discharging her cargo into the other ships, her hull, "being very leaky, was sold for 575 Dutch dollars to Captain John Opie, of the *Oley* frigate, lately arrived from London."

The Dutch were naturally not at all anxious to assist English ships in this part of the world; and it was the 8th of July, "after a long correspondence and many dilatory answers," before Rogers got leave from "the General" at Batavia to refit and careen at Horn Island, about three leagues to the northward of their present anchorage. He by no means suffering them to "careen at Umrest where all the Dutch ships are cleaned." This was a great grievance to Captain Rogers, especially as at Batavia he was not in a position to strengthen the Saxon of his despatches by any allusion to his six-pounders.

That he did what he could in a leaky ship to keep his powder dry at this time is, however, shown by an entry in the *Duke's* log, "that in rummaging one day in the powder room we found a leak three or four foot under water which we did our best to stop." While before arriving at Batavia the ten guns, which had been "struck down into the hold," at sea, were got up and mounted. This hoisting in and out of a frigate's hold of ten cannon as wanted, reads oddly in these days of heavy guns.

The forty sail Rogers found lying in Batavia Road were, nearly all Dutch, and during his stay there of four months only five other English ships touched at the port.

"Though about ten years past, an earthquake," Rogers tells us, "broke down part of the mountains, and rendered the canals in and about Batavia less commodious than formerly," his account of the place reminds one greatly of some stately sedate old Dutch City of today.

---

2. Captain Woodes Rogers not only lived to write his travels, but afterwards had charge of a naval squadron, sent to extirpate the pirates who infested the West Indies. He died in 1732, just a year after the death of Defoe.

"Situated," as he says, "in a bay, in which are seventeen Islands which so break the sea as to render the road safe though large. The banks of the canals are faced with stone on both sides as far as the boom, which is shut every night at 9 o'clock and guarded by soldiers. All the streets run in straight lines and are above thirty foot broad on each side clear of the canals and paved next the houses with bricks. All the streets are well built, fifteen of them having canals crossed by fifty-six bridges,—the country-seats and buildings round the City are generally neat, and well contrived, with handsom gardens adorned with springs, fountains and statues.

"The Cross-Church is a fine structure built of stone and very neat inside; there are also Hospitals, Spin-houses, and Rasp-houses as in Amsterdam, with all other public buildings equal to most cities in Europe. The Govenour's palace or castle, is of brick, large and well built, the great hall hung with bright armour, ensignes, flags, etc. taken by the Dutch here; it has four gates, well defended, the whole surrounded with ditches, and the works mounted with brass canon, as are the bastions of the town, with block-houses within the walls, so that they can fire upon mutineers as well as upon an enemy without.

"The outworks of the town, 4 leagues distance, are made of earth surrounded with ditches and quick-set hedges, which render them arbours for beauty, some of them faced with brick. The Govenour-General lives here in as great splendour as a king: he has a train and guards, a troop of horse, and a company of foot with halberts in liveries of yellow satin adorned with silver laces and fringes to attend his coach when he goes abroad."

Rogers concludes by saying, "it would be too tedious to describe all the remarkable things I saw in Batavia; for I was perfectly surprised when I came hither to see such a noble City, and Europeans so well settled in the Indies; having all necessaries for building and careening ships as well as in Europe, and officers as regular as in Her Majestie's Yards; whereas we have nothing like it in India.

"They keep their natives much in awe, but are favourable to the Chinese, who pay great rents for their shops, being about 8000 of them who pay the Dutch a dollar a head a month for liberty to wear their hair, which they are not allowed at home since they were conquered by the Tartars."

Owing to "some unwholesome water drunk by his crew while careening at Horn Island," Rogers lost several men here by fever, &c., and to replace them and others, who, tempted maybe by the price of *arrack*,[3] ran from the ships at this time, thirty-four Dutch sailors were shipped before sailing. Rogers must have known something of sailors and their ways, but even he expresses surprise at men deserting so late in the voyage, and losing their hard-earned share of prize-money, or, as he calls it, "plunder;" perhaps, however, in the case of the *Duke's* men, the prospect of constant work at the pumps had something to do with their leaving her.

The *Duke, Dutchess*, and *Batchelor*, did not actually take their "departure from Java Head" until October 4th, and it was the 27th of December before they "came up with Cape Falso and by noon were abreast of the Cape of Good Hope and saw the Table Land." During this three months' voyage, Rogers says, "nothing remarkable happened, except that on the 31st of October the *Duke*, having three feet of water in her, and her pumps choaked, we fired guns for our consorts to come to our relief, but had just sucked her" (*i.e.*, pumped her dry) "as the *Dutchess* came up."

"During the whole of this voyage," Rogers says, "he remained very thin and weak, as his ship did leaky," and the day after anchoring in Table Bay, "they buried Mr. Ware, chief surgeon, with naval honours as usual; being a very honest useful man, and good surgeon, bred up at Leyden in the study of phisick as well as surgery."

They lost also while at the Cape another important officer, in the person of Mr. Vanburgh; who in the early part of the cruise, as the *Duke's* agent, more than once gave Rogers trouble in his negotiations about plunder, &c.

The expenses of ships in commission could not have been great in Rogers' time, or they would have entirely swallowed any profits, even of a privateering cruise, due to the owners, owing to the length of time the vessels lay idle at anchorages such as Batavia Roads and Table Bay. For though the *Duke* and her consorts arrived at the Cape on the 27th of December, 1710, it was April, 1711, before they sailed for England in company with sixteen Dutch East Indiamen and six English ships. Rogers was anxious himself not to have waited for the convoy of these ships. "Thinking we should loose too much time by staying for them, and the benefit of their convoy to Holland; which would not only be out of the way, but very tedious and chargeable, while having large quantities of decaying goods on board, the time

---

3. Rogers speaks of shipping while at Batavia "half a leaguer of Spelman's *neep*, or the best sort of *arrack*." Is the modern term "nip of spirit" derived from this word neep?

lost in waiting for the Dutch at the Cape might be better spent in Brazil, where we could lie in little danger from an enemy and vend our goods at great rates; sailing thence to Bristol through the North channel with the summer before us.

"Keeping in the latitude of 55 or 56 degrees for two or three hundred leagues before getting the length" (*i.e.* longitude) "of the north of Ireland, and by that means avoiding the track of an enemy." But though Rogers "earnestly pressed, that if they would not agree to this, one of the privateers might take a run alone, and the other keep with the *Batchelor* and Dutch fleet," the majority was against the thing, and thought it safer to go home altogether under convoy of the Dutch than run any risk of losing their rich prize by meeting an enemy between the Cape and home.

Much of the officers' time during their long stay at the Cape was spent ashore holding sales of prize goods to the Dutch settlers; and among other things so disposed of, mention is particularly made of twelve negroes. Rogers also wrote to his owners from here telling them "of his safe arrival with the Acapulco ship, now called the *Batchelor* frigate mounted 20 great guns, and 200 brass *pattereroes*, with 116 men; a firm ship; and that the *Duke* and *Dutchess*, being fitted with everything necessary, only waited for the fleet which was expected to sail about the end of March."

Including the *Duke*, *Dutchess*, and *Batchelor*, a fleet of twenty-five armed ships was now ready to sail under the command of a Dutch flag, vice, and rear admiral. For though really only armed merchantmen, the commanders of these Dutch Indiamen, most of which were a thousand tons, took the rank and state of officers in the Dutch navy. And it must have been a picturesque scene in Table Bay, when at daybreak on the 5th of April "the Flag hoisted a blue ensign, loosed his foretopsail, and fired a gun as the signal to unmoor." In doing which on board the *Duke*, Rogers says, "our cable rubbed against the oakum, which for a time had partially stopped the leak, and occasioned his ship to be as leaky as ever, after having been indifferent tight for some time." As soon as the fleet was under weigh, the captains of the English vessels were signalled to go on board the flag-ship, to receive their order of sailing, &c., "which were very particular and obligatory to be punctually observed."

A voyage from the Cape to the Texel, even by the direct route up the British Channel, was a long one in those days for a fleet of this size, touching nowhere, and with over 5,000 men to feed; but the course they steered, away across the Atlantic to the westward of the Azores, and then north-eastward as far as the Shetlands, almost doubled the length of it. The squadron crossed the line on the 14th of May, "being the eighth time we have done so," says Rogers, "in our course round the world." This was thirty-eight days after leaving the Cape, giving a mean speed of rather more than three miles an hour.

The Spanish ship, the *Batchelor*, seems to have been the dullest sailer among them, for Rogers speaks of often taking her in tow, and of the Dutch admiral's "civility in allowing her to keep ahead of the fleet at night, which he would not permit any other ship to do." No collisions or disasters of any sort are recorded during the whole of this long voyage, the monotony of which was varied on the 15th of June by an entertainment on board the flag-ship to the skippers of the English and some of the Dutch ships, "when the good humour of the Admiral soon made all the company understand each other without a linguist." While on reaching latitude 51 north, thick foggy weather prevailed for many days, "during which the Flag-ship fired two guns every half hour, each ship answering with one, which consumed a great deal of powder, but by the noise of the guns it was easy to keep company, though often so thick that we could not see three ship's lengths" (equal to about one now).

Greatly to Rogers' admiration, the Dutchmen, being good ship's husbands, spent most of this time in scraping and cleaning their ships, bending new sails, &c., "so that they look as if newly come out of Holland;" and as they drew nearer home, and the chance of meeting an enemy increased, "the three admirals halled down their flags, and. to appear more like men of war hoisted pennants at their maintop mast-heads."

Evidently men like these three Dutch admirals were as much at home, if not as happy, afloat as ashore, if indeed a change from floating securely a few feet above the sea level to land many feet below it. could be called being ashore.

How many of those who today rattle about Holland by rail, and admire the stately well-to-do look of old Dutch cities and towns, give a thought to these sedate fleets of sailing Indiamen, in which the wealth that built and kept the sea from swallowing them every higher tide than usual was slowly but surely carried two hundred years ago; or know that shipping, moving then some five miles an hour under sail, actually paid its owners better than now, though driven by the feverish beat of steam round the world at fifteen knots. Soon after making Fair Island, near the Shetlands, on the 16th of July, Rogers says, "We fell in with the Dutch *men of war*, with the exception of one or two that remained cruising with the fishing doggers off the northeast of Shetland, where having little wind we lay by, the boats from the land coming to and fro all night and supplyd us with what they had, being poor people who live by fishing."

The whole squadron, now in convoy of the men-of war, with a small breeze, turned south again down the North Sea, and after seven days "crossed the bar, and anchored at 5 p.m. of the 23rd of July at the Texel in Holland, the Dutchmen," says Rogers, "firing all the guns for joy at their arrival in their own country, which they very affectionately call Fatherland." The cruise of the *Duke* and *Duchess* was virtually ended when they anchored in the Texel Roads, where they were met by some of the owners from England. But many delays occurred before they were ready to sail again, with some East India ships for London, in convoy of the *Essex, Canterbury, Meday,* and *Dunwich* men-of-war; so that it was October 14th before the last entry in Woodes Rogers' log was made, "that this day, at 11 of the clock, we and our Consorts and prize got up to Eriff, where we came to an anchor, which ends our long and fatiguing voyage."

THE OLD SHIP'S BELFRY

Appendix

A Receipt for a Sea Fight

The art of naval warfare has so greatly changed since the following prescription for chasing, fighting, and taking a 60-gun ship was written in Rogers's time, that it is really doubtful whether any definite rules for a sea fight could be given today. But in his time such matters appear to have been as well understood as the making of a bowl of good punch was. So, at any rate, we are taught by the author of "a collection of sundry pleasant and critical questions in navigation and the fighting of ships, for the improvement and diversion of the learner in his spare hours."

The writer of which tells us "he has had twenty-years' experience at sea as mate, master, and sworn teacher of the mathematicks to the gentlemen volunteers in Her Majestie's Royal Navy." He begins his instructions with the right methods of handling a ship in various kinds of weather, from the first change for the worse, "when the wind becometh fresh and frisking," until "it bloweth a storm with a very hollow grown sea." But the storm being past, the author says cheerfully, "Let us turn to windward," which soon brings his ship "into a good latitude and her proper station;" where the young officer is advised "to hand his topsails, farthel (or furl) the foresail and main-sail, trail up the mizen, and lie his ship a hull" (under bare poles) "until fortune appear upon the horizon;" a man being sent at the same time "to the maintop masthead "to look out for her in the shape of "any ships that have been nipt with the last northerly winds."

Like the big salmon of the literary fisherman, a sail is soon sighted, "A brave lusty ship of sixty guns. So much the better," says the writer, "for though we have but fifty, the enemy hath more goods in his hold, and it blows a brave chasing gale. Therefor let us set spritsails, spritsail-topsails, flying jib, and top-gallants; and as we raise her apace we shall

be up with her in three glasses" (half-hourglasses). It sounds strange in these days of monster iron-clads to read that during a chase in a fifty-gun ship the crew were "ordered aft to remain quiet there, as the ship will steer better being too much by the head."

The enemy soon goes about, and is immediately followed by the young beginner. The chase, "being a foul ship," (*i.e.* covered with weeds, barnacles, &c.), he gets to windward of her, and is advised to keep there, with "his enemy under his lee."

The gunner is now ordered "to see his guns all clear, and that nothing pester the decks." The hammocks being stowed round the bulwarks fore and aft in the nettings, the order is given to "down with all bulkheads" (cabin partitions, &c.)"that may hinder us or hurt with splinters;" and the gunner is asked, "whether there be good store of cartridges ready filled, and shot in the garlands" (racks for ball on deck) "between the guns and round the masts and hatches." He is also to see that "rammers, sponges, ladles, priming-irons, horns, lin-stocks, wads, swabs, and tubs of water, are all in place;" and that when engaged, "the guns be well loaded with cross-bar and langrel" (old nails and bolts tied in bundles to cut an enemy's rigging), "and that the blunderbusses, musketoons, pistoles, cutlashes, poleaxes, half-pikes, &c., are in readiness, and that the *patereroes*" (swivel guns) "and stock-fowlers in the round tops, have their chambers full of good powder, with bags of small shot" (bullets) "to load them, in order to clear the deck in case of the enemy boarding."

The men are then called to quarters; and, escape being impossible, the chase shortens sail, and "puts aboard the white French ensign," which is saluted with a cheer, and a remark, "that though a larger ship and full of men, we shall match her, for our colours are St. George's" Then comes a neat little oration, headed *The Captain's Speech*.

"Gentlemen, We are maintained by Her Majestie Queen Anne, and our country, to do our endeavours to keep the sea from Her Maj-estie's enemies, piracy, and robbers; and 'tis our fortune to meet this ship. Therefore I desire you, in Her Majestie's name, and for your own countrie's honour, that every man behave himself like an Englishman, and courageous to observe the word of command and do his best endeavour. So, committing ourselves and cause into God's hand, every man to his quarter, and God be with us and grant us victory!"

This speech is at once followed by an order to the ship's musi-cians of "Up noise of trumpets, and hail our prize," which the French ship "answereth again with her trumpets." Which preliminaries of the old naval duel being over, the gunner is warned "to hold fast and not fire until fairly alongside of him, and within musket-shot." The time arrived, the guns are run out with the command, "Give him a broadside, a volley of small arms, and a huzza." After which the men are encouraged with, "Well done, my hearts? The enemy returns the compliment. What cheer, is all well betwixt decks? Yea, yea, only he hath raked us through and through.

"No fear, 'tis our turn next. Edge toward him, and give not fire until we are within pistol-shot. Port your helm, he plies his small shot.—Come, boys, load and fire our small arms briskly,—Hold fast, gunner; right your helm, and run up alongside. Starboard a little.— Now a broadside, gunner.—That was well done; this one hath thinned their, decks of men, but his small arms did gall us. Clap some case and partridge into the guns now loading. Brace-to the fore topsail that we shoot not ahead of him. He lies broad-off to bring his other broadside to bear. Starboard hard! Trim your topsails. He fires his starboard broadside, and pours in small shot.—Give no fire till he falls off, that he may receive our full broadside. Steady!—Port a little.—Fire!— Huzza! Cheerly, my mates, his foremast is by the board; that broadside did execution.

"He bears away to stop leaks; the day will be ours! Keeps her thus.—Port, port hard! Bear up and give him our starboard broad-side. Load with double-head round and case-shot. Yea, yea; port, make ready to board; have lashers and grapplings ready, with able men to tend 'em. Well steered; edge toward him, and when you fire bring your guns to bear right among his men with the case-shot. Fire!— Starboard, well done my hearts! they lie heads and points aboard the prize. Board him bravely. Enter, enter. Are you fast lashed? Yea, yea. Cut up his decks, ply your hand-grenades. They cry quarter!—Good: quarter is granted providing you lay down arms; open your hatches, haul down all sails and furl them. Loose the lashings, and we will sheer off and hoist out our boats; but if you offer to fire or make sail again, expect no quarter for your lives." Boats are then lowered, and the captain, officers, and part of the crew of the prize taken on board the young beginner's ship.

So much for the attack and capture of a vessel at sea in those days. In case, however, "the reader be curious to learn" something of the measures taken by merchantmen in Rogers' time to beat off an enemy, he is referred to "Defensive Sea Fighting" in Park's *Art of Fighting in Merchant Ships.*

From the "Table of Gunnery" given below it would seem that our ancestors' guns were stronger or their powder weaker than ours, the weight of a charge of powder given in it in some cases exceeding half the weight of the shot:—

	Weight of Gun.	Weight of Shot.		Weight of Powder.		Range Point blank.	Range Extreme.
	lbs.	lbs.	oz.	lbs.	oz.	yards.	yards.
Cannon Royal	8,000	58	0	23	0	300	3,000
Demi-cannon	5,200	32	0	15	0	300	3,000
24 Pounder	4,800	24	0	11	0	300	3,000
12 Pounder	3,000	12	0	8	0	295	2,900
Saker	1,500	5	4	4	0	250	2,500
Faucon	750	2	8	1	8	200	2,000

A TABLE OF GUNNERY

SOME OBSERVATIONS ON FINDING THE LONGITUDE AT SEA

For want of correct timekeepers, a ship's longitude was, in time bf Queen Anne and for some time afterwards, an unsolved problem. But in the *Compleat Modern Navigator's Tutor, or The whole Art of Navigation*, published by one Joshua Kelly, of "Broad Street Wapping near Wapping New-stairs," in 1720, we are taught "five of the most rational ways of finding it." The learner is advised, however, "not to confide too much in them, or to omit any of the methods of a sea journal or other precautions to preserve a ship when she nears land." Among these methods eclipses of the moon and Jupiter's satellites of course come first. But of the first of these methods we are told that "it would be accurate and useful if we could have an eclipse of the moon every night," and of the second, that "the impractibility of managing a telescope twelve or fourteen feet long in the tossing rolling motion of a ship at sea, surrounds it with difficulties scarce to be remedied."

The craving of these old navigators for some form of good sea timekeeper is shown by Kelly's suggestion for finding the longitude by what he calls "automatas, or unerring clocks or watches," or even by "hour-glasses," directions being given for "preparing and using a very perfect and true-running sand glass, which may precisely run twenty-four hours without error, to be set exactly at noon on leaving the land; which glass upon being run out, is to be turned instantly every day, not losing any time in the turning of it; and so having very warily kept the said glass 'til you think good to make an observation at noon, and having in readiness an half hour, minute, and half minute glass, you may thereby know exactly how much the twenty- four hour-glass is before or after the ship's time; the difference being your longitude, east or west, according as the time by the sun is afore or after the time by the glass."

Navigation by account, or dead reckoning, has changed little since Kelly's time. Indeed, the use of the chronometer and the perfection of the modern sextant has almost superseded it except in the case of small coasters, &c.

But in Kelly and Woodes Rogers' days the log chip, reel, line, and half minute glass were the mariner's sole means of finding his longitude, or distance, sailed east or west.

Steam and patent logs have much simplified such calculation, which required many corrections not only for leeway but for errors in the log line and glass; "Shortness of the knots in a line," says Kelly, "being on the safer side, that a ship be not ahead of her reckoning; it being better to look for land before we come at it than to *be ashoar before we expect it.*"

SEA STORMS, ANCIENT AND MODERN

Are the storms at sea of this century heavier than those of the time of Queen Anne? is a question one can hardly help asking after studying the logs of the *Duke* and *Dutchess*e during their three years' cruise. Judging from Rogers's account, the whole of this period must have been one of remarkably fine weather at sea, even in the latitude of Cape Horn, as compared with the tempests torn to tatters which we constantly fall in with in the sea stories of today,

Or perhaps Captain Woodes Rogers was of that old type of happy sea-dog for whom the song was written in which Jack "pities them poor folk ashore," when a storm comes on? Or perhaps "life on the ocean wave" in his time was really not so terrible for sailormen as it is now? These questions are not easily answered, for even among comparatively recent sea-writers, such as Marryat and Dana, life afloat, though not described as all smooth sailing, is never described as all hurricane and hurly-burly. Like a true seaman Marryat delights to draw pictures of men at home on the sea, and well able to contend with wind and wave, rather than write of ships with sails torn to shreds, and crews taking to drink as soon as they are caught in a close-reefed topsail breeze off Cape Horn.

Steam, no doubt, has much to answer for in having increased, rather than diminished, the apparent terrors of bad weather at sea; causing writers who draw their experiences of storms from the decks óf long narrow ships driven six or seven knots in the teeth of a gale, or from some top-heavy mastless mass of iron and steel washed by the sea of even a summer gale like a half-tide rock, to form exaggerated ideas of tempests, and the behaviour of well-handled sailing craft in the same weathers. A steamer plunges into a head-sea in a blundering sort of way, wallowing from side to side as she does so, and shipping water to port or starboard in the most uncertain manner.

The power which drives the great hull against the rolling masses of water seems to have no sympathy with either the ship or waves; and drenched from stem to stern, the vessel reels and staggers on her way, kept only to her work by careful use of helm. Now, the sailing vessel, meets a head-sea, when lying-to under easy canvas, as though she knew just what to do with it. She is at one, so to speak, with the whole matter. Her long tapering spars act pendulum-like, checking all sudden or jerky rolling; and as long as a stitch of canvas can be set she meets the waves in a give-and-take way reminding one of the *soft answer that turneth away wrath.*

Again modern describers of sea-storms seem to forget, that on board well-found ships, things are not. merely fitted for use in fair weather, but to bear the strain of bad weathers; and that loss of canvas and spars at sea was, and is, looked upon as a matter of negligence; so much so that in the navy most of these losses had to be made good by the officer in command. And one seldom heard in old sea stories of cordage left to rattle and shriek, or sails to bang about and explode like cannon in the hands of real seamen. In fact, after once the canvas was reduced to its lowest, a head gale in a soling vessel was less noisy than the same wind on shore among trees or houses; while down below the noise of the weather was not to be compared with the rattle and rumble of a gale inside a house.

In the case of a sudden squall striking a ship after a spell of fine weather, or just after leaving port, no doubt a few loose things might fetch away, and give young sailors or passengers the notion that everything was going topsy-turvy; but after a short spell of really hard weather, things soon get into place at sea, and, so far as officers and crew are concerned, the routine of sea life goes on as monotonously as in more moderate weather. Even in that nobly simple story of disaster at sea, told of St. Paul, the approach of the catastrophe is unattended by noise; there is none of the confusion and shrieking of cordage that mark the stagey shipwreck of modern fiction

Nor did those old shipmen yield the loss of their ship without a good fight; but after sounding twice they cast four anchors out of the stern and quietly watched for the day. After which, the ship's head being already shoreward, the rudder bands were loosed, and a final effort was made to save their vessel by running for a creek; until falling into a place where two seas met, the ship struck, and some on planks, and some on broken pieces of the wreck, all got safe to shore.

THE OLD SEA CLOCK

LEONAUR

ALSO FROM LEONAUR
AVAILABLE IN SOFTCOVER OR HARDCOVER WITH DUST JACKET

THE 2ND MAORI WAR: 1860-1861 *by Robert Carey*—The Second Maori War, or First Taranaki War, one more bloody instalment of the conflicts between European settlers and the indigenous Maori people.

A JOURNAL OF THE SECOND SIKH WAR *by Daniel A. Sandford*—The Experiences of an Ensign of the 2nd Bengal European Regiment During the Campaign in the Punjab, India, 1848-49.

THE LIGHT INFANTRY OFFICER *by John H. Cooke*—The Experiences of an Officer of the 43rd Light Infantry in America During the War of 1812.

BUSHVELDT CARBINEERS *by George Witton*—The War Against the Boers in South Africa and the 'Breaker' Morant Incident.

LAKE'S CAMPAIGNS IN INDIA *by Hugh Pearse*—The Second Anglo Maratha War, 1803-1807.

BRITAIN IN AFGHANISTAN 1: THE FIRST AFGHAN WAR 1839-42 *by Archibald Forbes*—From invasion to destruction-a British military disaster.

BRITAIN IN AFGHANISTAN 2: THE SECOND AFGHAN WAR 1878-80 *by Archibald Forbes*—This is the history of the Second Afghan War-another episode of British military history typified by savagery, massacre, siege and battles.

UP AMONG THE PANDIES *by Vivian Dering Majendie*—Experiences of a British Officer on Campaign During the Indian Mutiny, 1857-1858.

MUTINY: 1857 *by James Humphries*—Authentic Voices from the Indian Mutiny-First Hand Accounts of Battles, Sieges and Personal Hardships.

BLOW THE BUGLE, DRAW THE SWORD *by W. H. G. Kingston*—The Wars, Campaigns, Regiments and Soldiers of the British & Indian Armies During the Victorian Era, 1839-1898.

WAR BEYOND THE DRAGON PAGODA *by Major J. J. Snodgrass*—A Personal Narrative of the First Anglo-Burmese War 1824 - 1826.

THE HERO OF ALIWAL *by James Humphries*—The Campaigns of Sir Harry Smith in India, 1843-1846, During the Gwalior War & the First Sikh War.

ALL FOR A SHILLING A DAY *by Donald F. Featherstone*—The story of H.M. 16th, the Queen's Lancers During the first Sikh War 1845-1846.

LEONAUR

ALSO FROM LEONAUR
AVAILABLE IN SOFTCOVER OR HARDCOVER WITH DUST JACKET

THE FALL OF THE MOGHUL EMPIRE OF HINDUSTAN *by H. G. Keene*—By the beginning of the nineteenth century, as British and Indian armies under Lake and Wellesley dominated the scene, a little over half a century of conflict brought the Moghul Empire to its knees.

LADY SALE'S AFGHANISTAN *by Florentia Sale*—An Indomitable Victorian Lady's Account of the Retreat from Kabul During the First Afghan War.

THE CAMPAIGN OF MAGENTA AND SOLFERINO 1859 *by Harold Carmichael Wylly*—The Decisive Conflict for the Unification of Italy.

FRENCH'S CAVALRY CAMPAIGN *by J. G. Maydon*—A Special Correspondent's View of British Army Mounted Troops During the Boer War.

CAVALRY AT WATERLOO *by Sir Evelyn Wood*—British Mounted Troops During the Campaign of 1815.

THE SUBALTERN *by George Robert Gleig*—The Experiences of an Officer of the 85th Light Infantry During the Peninsular War.

NAPOLEON AT BAY, 1814 *by F. Loraine Petre*—The Campaigns to the Fall of the First Empire.

NAPOLEON AND THE CAMPAIGN OF 1806 *by Colonel Vachée*—The Napoleonic Method of Organisation and Command to the Battles of Jena & Auerstädt.

THE COMPLETE ADVENTURES IN THE CONNAUGHT RANGERS *by William Grattan*—The 88th Regiment during the Napoleonic Wars by a Serving Officer.

BUGLER AND OFFICER OF THE RIFLES *by William Green & Harry Smith*—With the 95th (Rifles) during the Peninsular & Waterloo Campaigns of the Napoleonic Wars.

NAPOLEONIC WAR STORIES *by Sir Arthur Quiller-Couch*—Tales of soldiers, spies, battles & sieges from the Peninsular & Waterloo campaingns.

CAPTAIN OF THE 95TH (RIFLES) *by Jonathan Leach*—An officer of Wellington's sharpshooters during the Peninsular, South of France and Waterloo campaigns of the Napoleonic wars.

RIFLEMAN COSTELLO *by Edward Costello*—The adventures of a soldier of the 95th (Rifles) in the Peninsular & Waterloo Campaigns of the Napoleonic wars.

LEONAUR

ALSO FROM LEONAUR

AVAILABLE IN SOFTCOVER OR HARDCOVER WITH DUST JACKET

AT THEM WITH THE BAYONET *by Donald F. Featherstone*—The first Anglo-Sikh War 1845-1846.

STEPHEN CRANE'S BATTLES *by Stephen Crane*—Nine Decisive Battles Recounted by the Author of 'The Red Badge of Courage'.

THE GURKHA WAR *by H. T. Prinsep*—The Anglo-Nepalese Conflict in North East India 1814-1816.

FIRE & BLOOD *by G. R. Gleig*—The burning of Washington & the battle of New Orleans, 1814, through the eyes of a young British soldier.

SOUND ADVANCE! *by Joseph Anderson*—Experiences of an officer of HM 50th regiment in Australia, Burma & the Gwalior war.

THE CAMPAIGN OF THE INDUS *by Thomas Holdsworth*—Experiences of a British Officer of the 2nd (Queen's Royal) Regiment in the Campaign to Place Shah Shuja on the Throne of Afghanistan 1838 - 1840.

WITH THE MADRAS EUROPEAN REGIMENT IN BURMA *by John Butler*—The Experiences of an Officer of the Honourable East India Company's Army During the First Anglo-Burmese War 1824 - 1826.

IN ZULULAND WITH THE BRITISH ARMY *by Charles L. Norris-Newman*—The Anglo-Zulu war of 1879 through the first-hand experiences of a special correspondent.

BESIEGED IN LUCKNOW *by Martin Richard Gubbins*—The first Anglo-Sikh War 1845-1846.

A TIGER ON HORSEBACK *by L. March Phillips*—The Experiences of a Trooper & Officer of Rimington's Guides - The Tigers - during the Anglo-Boer war 1899 - 1902.

SEPOYS, SIEGE & STORM *by Charles John Griffiths*—The Experiences of a young officer of H.M.'s 61st Regiment at Ferozepore, Delhi ridge and at the fall of Delhi during the Indian mutiny 1857.

CAMPAIGNING IN ZULULAND *by W. E. Montague*—Experiences on campaign during the Zulu war of 1879 with the 94th Regiment.

THE STORY OF THE GUIDES *by G.J. Younghusband*—The Exploits of the Soldiers of the famous Indian Army Regiment from the northwest frontier 1847 - 1900.

LEONAUR

ALSO FROM LEONAUR
AVAILABLE IN SOFTCOVER OR HARDCOVER WITH DUST JACKET

ZULU:1879 *by D.C.F. Moodie & the Leonaur Editors*—The Anglo-Zulu War of 1879 from contemporary sources: First Hand Accounts, Interviews, Dispatches, Official Documents & Newspaper Reports.

THE RED DRAGOON *by W.J. Adams*—With the 7th Dragoon Guards in the Cape of Good Hope against the Boers & the Kaffir tribes during the 'war of the axe' 1843-48'.

THE RECOLLECTIONS OF SKINNER OF SKINNER'S HORSE *by James Skinner*—James Skinner and his 'Yellow Boys' Irregular cavalry in the wars of India between the British, Mahratta, Rajput, Mogul, Sikh & Pindarree Forces.

A CAVALRY OFFICER DURING THE SEPOY REVOLT *by A. R. D. Mackenzie*—Experiences with the 3rd Bengal Light Cavalry, the Guides and Sikh Irregular Cavalry from the outbreak to Delhi and Lucknow.

A NORFOLK SOLDIER IN THE FIRST SIKH WAR *by J W Baldwin*—Experiences of a private of H.M. 9th Regiment of Foot in the battles for the Punjab, India 1845-6.

TOMMY ATKINS' WAR STORIES: 14 FIRST HAND ACCOUNTS—Fourteen first hand accounts from the ranks of the British Army during Queen Victoria's Empire.

THE WATERLOO LETTERS *by H. T. Siborne*—Accounts of the Battle by British Officers for its Foremost Historian.

NEY: GENERAL OF CAVALRY VOLUME 1—1769-1799 *by Antoine Bulos*—The Early Career of a Marshal of the First Empire.

NEY: MARSHAL OF FRANCE VOLUME 2—1799-1805 *by Antoine Bulos*—The Early Career of a Marshal of the First Empire.

AIDE-DE-CAMP TO NAPOLEON *by Philippe-Paul de Ségur*—For anyone interested in the Napoleonic Wars this book, written by one who was intimate with the strategies and machinations of the Emperor, will be essential reading.

TWILIGHT OF EMPIRE *by Sir Thomas Ussher & Sir George Cockburn*—Two accounts of Napoleon's Journeys in Exile to Elba and St. Helena: Narrative of Events by Sir Thomas Ussher & Napoleon's Last Voyage: Extract of a diary by Sir George Cockburn.

PRIVATE WHEELER *by William Wheeler*—The letters of a soldier of the 51st Light Infantry during the Peninsular War & at Waterloo.

LEONAUR

ALSO FROM LEONAUR
AVAILABLE IN SOFTCOVER OR HARDCOVER WITH DUST JACKET

OFFICERS & GENTLEMEN *by Peter Hawker & William Graham*—Two Accounts of British Officers During the Peninsula War: Officer of Light Dragoons by Peter Hawker & Campaign in Portugal and Spain by William Graham .

THE WALCHEREN EXPEDITION *by Anonymous*—The Experiences of a British Officer of the 81st Regt. During the Campaign in the Low Countries of 1809.

LADIES OF WATERLOO *by Charlotte A. Eaton, Magdalene de Lancey & Juana Smith*—The Experiences of Three Women During the Campaign of 1815: Waterloo Days by Charlotte A. Eaton, A Week at Waterloo by Magdalene de Lancey & Juana's Story by Juana Smith.

JOURNAL OF AN OFFICER IN THE KING'S GERMAN LEGION *by John Frederick Hering*—Recollections of Campaigning During the Napoleonic Wars.

JOURNAL OF AN ARMY SURGEON IN THE PENINSULAR WAR *by Charles Boutflower*—The Recollections of a British Army Medical Man on Campaign During the Napoleonic Wars.

ON CAMPAIGN WITH MOORE AND WELLINGTON *by Anthony Hamilton*—The Experiences of a Soldier of the 43rd Regiment During the Peninsular War.

THE ROAD TO AUSTERLITZ *by R. G. Burton*—Napoleon's Campaign of 1805.

SOLDIERS OF NAPOLEON *by A. J. Doisy De Villargennes & Arthur Chuquet*—The Experiences of the Men of the French First Empire: Under the Eagles by A. J. Doisy De Villargennes & Voices of 1812 by Arthur Chuquet .

INVASION OF FRANCE, 1814 *by F. W. O. Maycock*—The Final Battles of the Napoleonic First Empire.

LEIPZIG—A CONFLICT OF TITANS *by Frederic Shoberl*—A Personal Experience of the 'Battle of the Nations' During the Napoleonic Wars, October 14th-19th, 1813.

SLASHERS *by Charles Cadell*—The Campaigns of the 28th Regiment of Foot During the Napoleonic Wars by a Serving Officer.

BATTLE IMPERIAL *by Charles William Vane*—The Campaigns in Germany & France for the Defeat of Napoleon 1813-1814.

SWIFT & BOLD *by Gibbes Rigaud*—The 60th Rifles During the Peninsula War.

LEONAUR

ALSO FROM LEONAUR

AVAILABLE IN SOFTCOVER OR HARDCOVER WITH DUST JACKET

ADVENTURES OF A YOUNG RIFLEMAN *by Johann Christian Maempel*—The Experiences of a Saxon in the French & British Armies During the Napoleonic Wars.

THE HUSSAR *by Norbert Landsheit & G. R. Gleig*—A German Cavalryman in British Service Throughout the Napoleonic Wars.

RECOLLECTIONS OF THE PENINSULA *by Moyle Sherer*—An Officer of the 34th Regiment of Foot—'The Cumberland Gentlemen'—on Campaign Against Napoleon's French Army in Spain.

MARINE OF REVOLUTION & CONSULATE *by Moreau de Jonnès*—The Recollections of a French Soldier of the Revolutionary Wars 1791-1804.

GENTLEMEN IN RED *by John Dobbs & Robert Knowles*—Two Accounts of British Infantry Officers During the Peninsular War Recollections of an Old 52nd Man by John Dobbs An Officer of Fusiliers by Robert Knowles.

CORPORAL BROWN'S CAMPAIGNS IN THE LOW COUNTRIES *by Robert Brown*—Recollections of a Coldstream Guard in the Early Campaigns Against Revolutionary France 1793-1795.

THE 7TH (QUEENS OWN) HUSSARS: Volume 2—1793-1815 *by C. R. B. Barrett*—During the Campaigns in the Low Countries & the Peninsula and Waterloo Campaigns of the Napoleonic Wars. Volume 2: 1793-1815.

THE MARENGO CAMPAIGN 1800 *by Herbert H. Sargent*—The Victory that Completed the Austrian Defeat in Italy.

DONALDSON OF THE 94TH—SCOTS BRIGADE *by Joseph Donaldson*—The Recollections of a Soldier During the Peninsula & South of France Campaigns of the Napoleonic Wars.

A CONSCRIPT FOR EMPIRE *by Philippe as told to Johann Christian Maempel*—The Experiences of a Young German Conscript During the Napoleonic Wars.

JOURNAL OF THE CAMPAIGN OF 1815 *by Alexander Cavalié Mercer*—The Experiences of an Officer of the Royal Horse Artillery During the Waterloo Campaign.

NAPOLEON'S CAMPAIGNS IN POLAND 1806-7 *by Robert Wilson*—The campaign in Poland from the Russian side of the conflict.

LEONAUR

ALSO FROM LEONAUR
AVAILABLE IN SOFTCOVER OR HARDCOVER WITH DUST JACKET

OMPTEDA OF THE KING'S GERMAN LEGION *by Christian von Ompteda*—A Hanoverian Officer on Campaign Against Napoleon.

LIEUTENANT SIMMONS OF THE 95TH (RIFLES) *by George Simmons*—Recollections of the Peninsula, South of France & Waterloo Campaigns of the Napoleonic Wars.

A HORSEMAN FOR THE EMPEROR *by Jean Baptiste Gazzola*—A Cavalryman of Napoleon's Army on Campaign Throughout the Napoleonic Wars.

SERGEANT LAWRENCE *by William Lawrence*—With the 40th Regt. of Foot in South America, the Peninsular War & at Waterloo.

CAMPAIGNS WITH THE FIELD TRAIN *by Richard D. Henegan*—Experiences of a British Officer During the Peninsula and Waterloo Campaigns of the Napoleonic Wars.

CAVALRY SURGEON *by S. D. Broughton*—On Campaign Against Napoleon in the Peninsula & South of France During the Napoleonic Wars 1812-1814.

MEN OF THE RIFLES *by Thomas Knight, Henry Curling & Jonathan Leach*—The Reminiscences of Thomas Knight of the 95th (Rifles) by Thomas Knight, Henry Curling's Anecdotes by Henry Curling & The Field Services of the Rifle Brigade from its Formation to Waterloo by Jonathan Leach.

THE ULM CAMPAIGN 1805 *by F. N. Maude*—Napoleon and the Defeat of the Austrian Army During the 'War of the Third Coalition'.

SOLDIERING WITH THE 'DIVISION' *by Thomas Garrety*—The Military Experiences of an Infantryman of the 43rd Regiment During the Napoleonic Wars.

SERGEANT MORRIS OF THE 73RD FOOT *by Thomas Morris*—The Experiences of a British Infantryman During the Napoleonic Wars-Including Campaigns in Germany and at Waterloo.

A VOICE FROM WATERLOO *by Edward Cotton*—The Personal Experiences of a British Cavalryman Who Became a Battlefield Guide and Authority on the Campaign of 1815.

NAPOLEON AND HIS MARSHALS *by J. T. Headley*—The Men of the First Empire.

LEONAUR

ALSO FROM LEONAUR
AVAILABLE IN SOFTCOVER OR HARDCOVER WITH DUST JACKET

COLBORNE: A SINGULAR TALENT FOR WAR *by John Colborne*—The Napoleonic Wars Career of One of Wellington's Most Highly Valued Officers in Egypt, Holland, Italy, the Peninsula and at Waterloo.

NAPOLEON'S RUSSIAN CAMPAIGN *by Philippe Henri de Segur*—The Invasion, Battles and Retreat by an Aide-de-Camp on the Emperor's Staff.

WITH THE LIGHT DIVISION *by John H. Cooke*—The Experiences of an Officer of the 43rd Light Infantry in the Peninsula and South of France During the Napoleonic Wars.

WELLINGTON AND THE PYRENEES CAMPAIGN VOLUME I: FROM VITORIA TO THE BIDASSOA *by F. C. Beatson*—The final phase of the campaign in the Iberian Peninsula.

WELLINGTON AND THE INVASION OF FRANCE VOLUME II: THE BIDASSOA TO THE BATTLE OF THE NIVELLE *by F. C. Beatson*—The final phase of the campaign in the Iberian Peninsula.

WELLINGTON AND THE FALL OF FRANCE VOLUME III: THE GAVES AND THE BATTLE OF ORTHEZ *by F. C. Beatson*—The final phase of the campaign in the Iberian Peninsula.

NAPOLEON'S IMPERIAL GUARD: FROM MARENGO TO WATERLOO *by J. T. Headley*—The story of Napoleon's Imperial Guard and the men who commanded them.

BATTLES & SIEGES OF THE PENINSULAR WAR *by W. H. Fitchett*—Corunna, Busaco, Albuera, Ciudad Rodrigo, Badajos, Salamanca, San Sebastian & Others.

SERGEANT GUILLEMARD: THE MAN WHO SHOT NELSON? *by Robert Guillemard*—A Soldier of the Infantry of the French Army of Napoleon on Campaign Throughout Europe.

WITH THE GUARDS ACROSS THE PYRENEES *by Robert Batty*—The Experiences of a British Officer of Wellington's Army During the Battles for the Fall of Napoleonic France, 1813 .

A STAFF OFFICER IN THE PENINSULA *by E. W. Buckham*—An Officer of the British Staff Corps Cavalry During the Peninsula Campaign of the Napoleonic Wars.

THE LEIPZIG CAMPAIGN: 1813—NAPOLEON AND THE "BATTLE OF THE NATIONS" *by F. N. Maude*—Colonel Maude's analysis of Napoleon's campaign of 1813 around Leipzig.

LEONAUR

ALSO FROM LEONAUR
AVAILABLE IN SOFTCOVER OR HARDCOVER WITH DUST JACKET

BUGEAUD: A PACK WITH A BATON *by Thomas Robert Bugeaud*—The Early Campaigns of a Soldier of Napoleon's Army Who Would Become a Marshal of France.

WATERLOO RECOLLECTIONS *by Frederick Llewellyn*—Rare First Hand Accounts, Letters, Reports and Retellings from the Campaign of 1815.

SERGEANT NICOL *by Daniel Nicol*—The Experiences of a Gordon Highlander During the Napoleonic Wars in Egypt, the Peninsula and France.

THE JENA CAMPAIGN: 1806 *by F. N. Maude*—The Twin Battles of Jena & Auerstadt Between Napoleon's French and the Prussian Army.

PRIVATE O'NEIL *by Charles O'Neil*—The recollections of an Irish Rogue of H. M. 28th Regt.—The Slashers—during the Peninsula & Waterloo campaigns of the Napoleonic war.

ROYAL HIGHLANDER *by James Anton*—A soldier of H.M 42nd (Royal) Highlanders during the Peninsular, South of France & Waterloo Campaigns of the Napoleonic Wars.

CAPTAIN BLAZE *by Elzéar Blaze*—Life in Napoleons Army.

LEJEUNE VOLUME 1 *by Louis-François Lejeune*—The Napoleonic Wars through the Experiences of an Officer on Berthier's Staff.

LEJEUNE VOLUME 2 *by Louis-François Lejeune*—The Napoleonic Wars through the Experiences of an Officer on Berthier's Staff.

CAPTAIN COIGNET *by Jean-Roch Coignet*—A Soldier of Napoleon's Imperial Guard from the Italian Campaign to Russia and Waterloo.

FUSILIER COOPER *by John S. Cooper*—Experiences in the 7th (Royal) Fusiliers During the Peninsular Campaign of the Napoleonic Wars and the American Campaign to New Orleans.

FIGHTING NAPOLEON'S EMPIRE *by Joseph Anderson*—The Campaigns of a British Infantryman in Italy, Egypt, the Peninsular & the West Indies During the Napoleonic Wars.

CHASSEUR BARRES *by Jean-Baptiste Barres*—The experiences of a French Infantryman of the Imperial Guard at Austerlitz, Jena, Eylau, Friedland, in the Peninsular, Lutzen, Bautzen, Zinnwald and Hanau during the Napoleonic Wars.

LEONAUR

ALSO FROM LEONAUR
AVAILABLE IN SOFTCOVER OR HARDCOVER WITH DUST JACKET

CAPTAIN COIGNET *by Jean-Roch Coignet*—A Soldier of Napoleon's Imperial Guard from the Italian Campaign to Russia and Waterloo.

HUSSAR ROCCA *by Albert Jean Michel de Rocca*—A French cavalry officer's experiences of the Napoleonic Wars and his views on the Peninsular Campaigns against the Spanish, British And Guerilla Armies.

MARINES TO 95TH (RIFLES) *by Thomas Fernyhough*—The military experiences of Robert Fernyhough during the Napoleonic Wars.

LIGHT BOB *by Robert Blakeney*—The experiences of a young officer in H.M 28th & 36th regiments of the British Infantry during the Peninsular Campaign of the Napoleonic Wars 1804 - 1814.

WITH WELLINGTON'S LIGHT CAVALRY *by William Tomkinson*—The Experiences of an officer of the 16th Light Dragoons in the Peninsular and Waterloo campaigns of the Napoleonic Wars.

SERGEANT BOURGOGNE *by Adrien Bourgogne*—With Napoleon's Imperial Guard in the Russian Campaign and on the Retreat from Moscow 1812 - 13.

SURTEES OF THE 95TH (RIFLES) *by William Surtees*—A Soldier of the 95th (Rifles) in the Peninsular campaign of the Napoleonic Wars.

SWORDS OF HONOUR *by Henry Newbolt & Stanley L. Wood*—The Careers of Six Outstanding Officers from the Napoleonic Wars, the Wars for India and the American Civil War.

ENSIGN BELL IN THE PENINSULAR WAR *by George Bell*—The Experiences of a young British Soldier of the 34th Regiment 'The Cumberland Gentlemen' in the Napoleonic wars.

HUSSAR IN WINTER *by Alexander Gordon*—A British Cavalry Officer during the retreat to Corunna in the Peninsular campaign of the Napoleonic Wars.

THE COMPLEAT RIFLEMAN HARRIS *by Benjamin Harris as told to and transcribed by Captain Henry Curling, 52nd Regt. of Foot*—The adventures of a soldier of the 95th (Rifles) during the Peninsular Campaign of the Napoleonic Wars.

THE ADVENTURES OF A LIGHT DRAGOON *by George Farmer & G.R. Gleig*—A cavalryman during the Peninsular & Waterloo Campaigns, in captivity & at the siege of Bhurtpore, India.

LEONAUR

ALSO FROM LEONAUR
AVAILABLE IN SOFTCOVER OR HARDCOVER WITH DUST JACKET

THE LIFE OF THE REAL BRIGADIER GERARD VOLUME 1—THE YOUNG HUSSAR 1782-1807 *by Jean-Baptiste De Marbot*—A French Cavalryman Of the Napoleonic Wars at Marengo, Austerlitz, Jena, Eylau & Friedland.

THE LIFE OF THE REAL BRIGADIER GERARD VOLUME 2—IMPERIAL AIDE-DE-CAMP 1807-1811 *by Jean-Baptiste De Marbot*—A French Cavalryman of the Napoleonic Wars at Saragossa, Landshut, Eckmuhl, Ratisbon, Aspern-Essling, Wagram, Busaco & Torres Vedras.

THE LIFE OF THE REAL BRIGADIER GERARD VOLUME 3—COLONEL OF CHASSEURS 1811-1815 *by Jean-Baptiste De Marbot*—A French Cavalryman in the retreat from Moscow, Lutzen, Bautzen, Katzbach, Leipzig, Hanau & Waterloo.

THE INDIAN WAR OF 1864 *by Eugene Ware*—The Experiences of a Young Officer of the 7th Iowa Cavalry on the Western Frontier During the Civil War.

THE MARCH OF DESTINY *by Charles E. Young & V. Devinny*—Dangers of the Trail in 1865 by Charles E. Young & The Story of a Pioneer by V. Devinny, two Accounts of Early Emigrants to Colorado.

CROSSING THE PLAINS *by William Audley Maxwell*—A First Hand Narrative of the Early Pioneer Trail to California in 1857.

CHIEF OF SCOUTS *by William F. Drannan*—A Pilot to Emigrant and Government Trains, Across the Plains of the Western Frontier.

THIRTY-ONE YEARS ON THE PLAINS AND IN THE MOUNTAINS *by William F. Drannan*—William Drannan was born to be a pioneer, hunter, trapper and wagon train guide during the momentous days of the Great American West.

THE INDIAN WARS VOLUNTEER *by William Thompson*—Recollections of the Conflict Against the Snakes, Shoshone, Bannocks, Modocs and Other Native Tribes of the American North West.

THE 4TH TENNESSEE CAVALRY *by George B. Guild*—The Services of Smith's Regiment of Confederate Cavalry by One of its Officers.

COLONEL WORTHINGTON'S SHILOH *by T. Worthington*—The Tennessee Campaign, 1862, by an Officer of the Ohio Volunteers.

FOUR YEARS IN THE SADDLE *by W. L. Curry*—The History of the First Regiment Ohio Volunteer Cavalry in the American Civil War.

LEONAUR

ALSO FROM LEONAUR
AVAILABLE IN SOFTCOVER OR HARDCOVER WITH DUST JACKET

LIFE IN THE ARMY OF NORTHERN VIRGINIA *by Carlton McCarthy*—The Observations of a Confederate Artilleryman of Cutshaw's Battalion During the American Civil War 1861-1865.

HISTORY OF THE CAVALRY OF THE ARMY OF THE POTOMAC *by Charles D. Rhodes*—Including Pope's Army of Virginia and the Cavalry Operations in West Virginia During the American Civil War.

CAMP-FIRE AND COTTON-FIELD *by Thomas W. Knox*—A New York Herald Correspondent's View of the American Civil War.

SERGEANT STILLWELL *by Leander Stillwell* —The Experiences of a Union Army Soldier of the 61st Illinois Infantry During the American Civil War.

STONEWALL'S CANNONEER *by Edward A. Moore*—Experiences with the Rockbridge Artillery, Confederate Army of Northern Virginia, During the American Civil War.

THE SIXTH CORPS *by George Stevens*—The Army of the Potomac, Union Army, During the American Civil War.

THE RAILROAD RAIDERS *by William Pittenger*—An Ohio Volunteers Recollections of the Andrews Raid to Disrupt the Confederate Railroad in Georgia During the American Civil War.

CITIZEN SOLDIER *by John Beatty*—An Account of the American Civil War by a Union Infantry Officer of Ohio Volunteers Who Became a Brigadier General.

COX: PERSONAL RECOLLECTIONS OF THE CIVIL WAR--VOLUME 1 *by Jacob Dolson Cox*—West Virginia, Kanawha Valley, Gauley Bridge, Cotton Mountain, South Mountain, Antietam, the Morgan Raid & the East Tennessee Campaign.

COX: PERSONAL RECOLLECTIONS OF THE CIVIL WAR--VOLUME 2 *by Jacob Dolson Cox*—Siege of Knoxville, East Tennessee, Atlanta Campaign, the Nashville Campaign & the North Carolina Campaign.

KERSHAW'S BRIGADE VOLUME 1 *by D. Augustus Dickert*—Manassas, Seven Pines, Sharpsburg (Antietam), Fredericksburg, Chancellorsville, Gettysburg, Chickamauga, Chattanooga, Fort Sanders & Bean Station.

KERSHAW'S BRIGADE VOLUME 2 *by D. Augustus Dickert*—At the wilderness, Cold Harbour, Petersburg, The Shenandoah Valley and Cedar Creek..

LEONAUR

ALSO FROM LEONAUR

AVAILABLE IN SOFTCOVER OR HARDCOVER WITH DUST JACKET

THE 9TH—THE KING'S (LIVERPOOL REGIMENT) IN THE GREAT WAR 1914 - 1918 *by Enos H. G. Roberts*—Mersey to mud—war and Liverpool men.

THE GAMBARDIER *by Mark Severn*—The experiences of a battery of Heavy artillery on the Western Front during the First World War.

FROM MESSINES TO THIRD YPRES *by Thomas Floyd*—A personal account of the First World War on the Western front by a 2/5th Lancashire Fusilier.

THE IRISH GUARDS IN THE GREAT WAR - VOLUME 1 *by Rudyard Kipling*—Edited and Compiled from Their Diaries and Papers—The First Battalion.

THE IRISH GUARDS IN THE GREAT WAR - VOLUME 1 *by Rudyard Kipling*—Edited and Compiled from Their Diaries and Papers—The Second Battalion.

ARMOURED CARS IN EDEN *by K. Roosevelt*—An American President's son serving in Rolls Royce armoured cars with the British in Mesopatamia & with the American Artillery in France during the First World War.

CHASSEUR OF 1914 *by Marcel Dupont*—Experiences of the twilight of the French Light Cavalry by a young officer during the early battles of the great war in Europe.

TROOP HORSE & TRENCH *by R.A. Lloyd*—The experiences of a British Lifeguardsman of the household cavalry fighting on the western front during the First World War 1914-18.

THE EAST AFRICAN MOUNTED RIFLES *by C.J. Wilson*—Experiences of the campaign in the East African bush during the First World War.

THE LONG PATROL *by George Berrie*—A Novel of Light Horsemen from Gallipoli to the Palestine campaign of the First World War.

THE FIGHTING CAMELIERS *by Frank Reid*—The exploits of the Imperial Camel Corps in the desert and Palestine campaigns of the First World War.

STEEL CHARIOTS IN THE DESERT *by S. C. Rolls*—The first world war experiences of a Rolls Royce armoured car driver with the Duke of Westminster in Libya and in Arabia with T.E. Lawrence.

WITH THE IMPERIAL CAMEL CORPS IN THE GREAT WAR *by Geoffrey Inchbald*—The story of a serving officer with the British 2nd battalion against the Senussi and during the Palestine campaign.

CPSIA information can be obtained
at www.ICGtesting.com
Printed in the USA
LVHW040815030119
602590LV00001B/157